STERLING
Test Prep

LAW ESSENTIALS

Conflict of Laws

Governing Law

3rd edition

This publication is designed to provide accurate and authoritative information regarding the subject matter covered. It is distributed with the understanding that the publisher, authors, or editors are not engaged in rendering legal or another professional service. If legal advice or other expert assistance is required, a competent professional's services should be sought.

Sterling Test Prep is not legally liable for mistakes, omissions, or inaccuracies in this publication's content. Sterling Test Prep does not guarantee that the user of this publication will pass the bar exam or achieve a performance level. Individual performance depends on many factors, including but not limited to the level of preparation, aptitude, and individual performance on test day.

3   2   1

ISBN-13: 979-8-8855700-3-9

Sterling Test Prep products are available at quantity discounts.

For more information, contact info@sterling–prep.com.

Sterling Test Prep
6 Liberty Square #11
Boston, MA 02109

©2022 Sterling Test Prep
Published by Sterling Test Prep
Printed in the U.S.A.

Customer Satisfaction Guarantee

Your feedback is important because we strive to provide the highest quality prep materials. Email us comments or suggestions.

info@sterling–prep.com

We reply to emails – check your spam folder

Thank you for choosing our book!

STERLING
Test Prep

Thousands of students use our study aids to prepare for law school exams and to pass the bar!

Passing the bar is essential for admission to practice law and launching your legal career.

This preparation guide describes the principles of substantive law governing the correct answers to exam questions. It was developed by legal professionals and law instructors who possess extensive credentials and have been admitted to practice law in several jurisdictions. The content is clearly presented and systematically organized for targeted preparation.

The performance on individual questions has been correlated with success or failure on the bar. By analyzing previously administered exams, the authors identified these predictive items and assembled the rules of law that govern the answers to questions tested. Learn the essential governing law to make fine-line distinctions among related principles and decide between tough choices on the exam. This knowledge is vital to excel in law school finals and pass the bar exam.

We look forward to being an essential part of your preparation and wish you great success in the legal profession!

Law Essentials series

Constitutional Law	Criminal Law and Criminal Procedure
Contracts	Business Associations
Evidence	Conflict of Laws
Real Property	Family Law
Torts	Secured Transactions
Civil Procedure	Trusts and Estates

Visit our Amazon store

Comprehensive Glossary of Legal Terms

Over 2,100 essential legal terms defined
and explained. An excellent reference
source for law students, practitioners and
readers seeking an understanding of legal
vocabulary and its application.

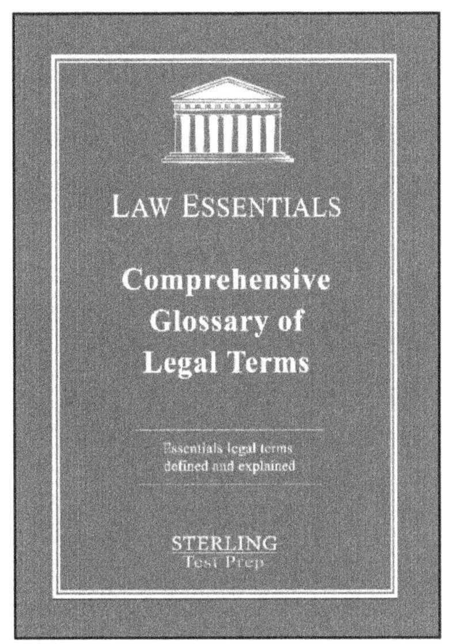

Landmark U.S. Supreme Court Cases: Essential Summaries

Learn important constitutional cases that
shaped American law. Understand how the
evolving needs of society intersect with the
U.S. Constitution. Short summaries of seminal
Supreme Court cases focused on issues and
holdings.

Visit our Amazon store

Table of Contents

CONFLICT OF LAWS GOVERNING LAW (*continued*)

CONFLICT OF LAWS GOVERNING LAW (*continued*)

CONFLICT OF LAWS GOVERNING LAW (*continued*)

EXAM INFORMATION, PREP & TEST-TAKING STRATEGIES (*continued*)

EXAM INFORMATION, PREP & TEST-TAKING STRATEGIES (*continued*)

APPENDIX (*continued*)

APPENDIX (*continued*)

Constitutional Amendments XI–XXVII (*continued*)

States' Rights Under the U.S. Constitution

Conflict of Laws
Governing Law

Conflict of Laws arises when there is a difference between the laws of two or more jurisdictions connected to the case. Conflict of laws considers what law should be applied to the case before the court. The outcome depends on which jurisdiction's law is used to resolve the issues in dispute. The process by which a court determines what law to apply is "characterization" or "classification."

The conflicting legal rules may come from U.S. federal law, state law, or the laws of other countries. Conflict of laws entails domicile, jurisdiction of the courts, choice of law, and recognition and enforcement of foreign judgments.

Conflict of Laws is not tested as a separate subject. It is generally tested on Civil Procedure and Family Law, and to a lesser extent on Trusts and Estates (decedent's estates specifically). Focus on highly tested Conflict of Laws issues to maximize your score. Frequently tested topics include the Klaxon doctrine, transfer of forum, recognition of marriage, full faith and credit, personal and real property within a decedents' estates.

Domicile

Privileges and immunities clause – citizens of each state are entitled to the privileges and immunities afforded the citizens of the state.

Full faith and credit – the courts of other states will honor the judgment of another court.

Recognition of judgment: analyzing the effect of a judgment in one jurisdiction rendered by another jurisdiction.

Establishing domicile

A person can have only one domicile (i.e., legal address).

2nd Restatement of Conflicts § 17 "Presence Under Compulsion" – people compelled to reside in a location (e.g., prisoners, military personnel) retain their prior domicile unless they intend to make the residence their domicile.

Legal capacity – needed to make a domicile of choice.

> Standard: the ability to fend for oneself.

> Individuals: physical presence and intent.

> Corporations: state of incorporation.

Two tests to establish domicile:

> 1) physical presence in that state (can be for a short time),

> 2) intent to remain for the foreseeable (indefinite) future.

Hague Convention – "domicile" is defined in terms of a person's permanent residence.

Objective standard – it does not focus on the party's intent.

Problematic since some people cannot reasonably be said to have a permanent residence (e.g., college students).

Intent for domicile

Residence (i.e., full- or part-time presence) is not synonymous with domicile.

Domicile is kept until another one is acquired.

Common law – must intend to remain indefinitely.

2nd Restatement and modern cases use intent to make the place home for some time (not forever).

The motive is irrelevant when determining the establishment of a new domicile except that it may supply evidence of intent.

Declarations of intent are not dispositive.

A defendant is always subject to the general jurisdiction of a court of domicile (i.e., nexus to government benefits, taxes, legal protections).

Domicile for legal proceedings

The domicile determines intestate succession to personal property.

The decedent is most familiar with the laws of their domicile.

Attorney consultations would most likely be conducted in the domicile.

The domicile state bears the burden of intestate distribution.

The domicile of the decedent is used to choose the law to be applied to determine the intestate succession of personal property.

Domicile at death determines which state gets estate taxes.

The law of the *situs* determines intestate succession to real property.

Conflicting domicile determinations – the states apply their standards for determining domicile and may separately rule that a party was domiciled in their respective state (a legal impossibility).

Dorrance v Martin et al. (1935) – two states imposed estate taxes after deciding that the decedent was domiciled in their respective state.

The imposition of multiple state estate taxes violates the due process clause only if the taxes exceed the value of the estate. To avoid additional tax, an intent to change domiciles should be done thoroughly and quickly.

Diversity actions – the parties must have different domiciles when the action is filed.

The courts may not recognize a change in domicile if it was done to create diversity or for tax advantages (only an artificial difference; no real intent).

Diversity jurisdiction aims to protect non-resident defendants from forum prejudice (a person who has artificially changed domiciles is not prejudiced).

Judicial jurisdiction

The definition of domicile may depend upon the purpose in a proceeding (e.g., statute).

Consider if the results achieved under traditional domicile rules are equitable and according to the statute's intent or other action.

Illegal immigrants acquire a new domicile for government benefits but not necessarily for family law matters (e.g., divorce).

Domicile by operation of law

If a person has no legal capacity to acquire a domicile of choice, they will be assigned a domicile by operation of law.

A person has one domicile at a time and does not lose it until they acquire a new one.

Being without a domicile anywhere is a legal impossibility.

2nd Restatement– a person can simultaneously have different domiciles for different purposes.

Domicile may be the headquarters of the person's personal and professional life.

The law of the forum determines domicile.

Original domicile: a person is presumed to have the domicile of their parents.

New domicile by choice

Establishing a new domicile requires legal capacity, physical presence, and a state of mind.

A person retains their domicile until a new one is perfected.

A mere intent to relinquish domicile without being present in the new one is insufficient.

English rule – one who gives up their domicile of choice regains their domicile of origin until a new one is attained.

American rule – a person retains their domicile until they acquire a new one.

Physical presence: the person must be present, even if briefly.

Domicile of child

Domicile by operation of law – imputed by statute regardless of the party's intent (e.g., parent/child).

An infant lacks the capacity to choose their domicile.

A child will have the domicile of their parents if they cannot make a choice.

If parents are divorced, domicile is that of a parent who has physical custody.

Married spouse

Marriage: domicile is the place of *celebration rule.*

Domicile of a spouse provides subject matter jurisdiction for a divorce.

Common law: a wife has the same domicile as a husband.

Modern view: each spouse may establish a domicile of choice.

Under common law, a husband's domicile was attributed to his wife, but it is only a presumption under modern law.

Jurisdiction of Courts

Types of jurisdiction

Legislative (prescriptive) jurisdiction is the outer limit of a state's power to apply its law, whether statutory or judge made.

Each court has the power to decide if it has jurisdiction over the parties & subject matter.

Recognition of judgment: analyzing the effect of a judgment in one jurisdiction rendered by another court.

Judicial jurisdiction – the power of a court to hear a dispute and render a valid judgment recognized by other courts.

Judicial jurisdiction requires:

> personal jurisdiction,
>
> subject matter jurisdiction, and
>
> *in rem* jurisdiction (authority over the thing)

Personal jurisdiction involves analyzing a court's assertion of the judicial power over parties.

Specific jurisdiction requires minimum contacts with the state. The suit arises out of or related to the defendant's contact with the forum state.

General jurisdiction involves suits not arising out of or related to the defendant's contacts with the forum state.

General jurisdiction requires sufficient contact with the state, which amounts to a continuous and systematic activity in the forum state.

Personal jurisdiction in state court

A defendant's contacts with the forum are such that the court may render a personal judgment against the defendant creating a judgment debt that other states may enforce under full faith and credit.

Personal jurisdiction requires minimum contacts with the state (e.g., the suit *arises out of* or *related to* the defendant's contact with the forum state).

Lack of personal jurisdiction is the classic form of a collateral attack.

Personal jurisdiction in federal courts

Absent congressional creation of federal jurisdiction (e.g., admiralty), a federal court is limited to the state court's jurisdictional reach where it sits.

The federal district court's power to assert personal jurisdiction is the same as the state court's power to assert personal jurisdiction where the federal district court sits.

For example, the District Court for Eastern TX analyzed the defendant's contact with Texas.

Traditional methods for courts to establish personal jurisdiction

Personal jurisdiction is established if the defendant is personally served in the forum state while voluntarily present in the state (purposely availing themselves to the benefits of the forum); no minimum contacts with the forum are required (transient jurisdiction).

Tag jurisdiction encourages forum shopping and could result in unfairness.

The defendant is domiciled in the forum state.

The rationale for jurisdiction – the defendant avails themself to the forum state's benefits.

The defendant consents to the court's exercise of personal jurisdiction.

A plaintiff consents to counterclaims by filing an action.

Forum selection clauses bind the parties to litigate in a forum (must be reasonable).

Consent to jurisdiction clause – vests a court with jurisdiction.

Waiver – the defendant fails to challenge jurisdiction.

The defendant appears specially but argues the merits – waives jurisdictional challenge.

Modern requirements for personal jurisdiction

Minimum contacts – the defendant must have minimum contacts with the forum state (e.g., *International Shoe*).

Foreseeability – the defendant should foresee being hauled into court in the forum.

Purposeful contacts or actions directed toward the forum.

Initiation – the defendant-initiated contact with the forum.

The greater the defendant's forum activities, the lower the need for the relatedness of the claim to the forum.

The defendant adjusted their primary conduct considering the forum's laws (usually applies to insurance cases).

The defendant derived benefits from the forum.

Fair play and substantial justice – subjecting the defendant to jurisdiction within the forum must meet with traditional notions of fair play and substantial justice:

> the interest of the forum state in hearing the case (involving its citizens),

> contrast *Asahi Metals* (1987), where the controversy was an indemnification action between two Japanese companies.

Overall fairness and reasonableness of exercising jurisdiction in the forum (defendant's burden of defending in the forum).

The plaintiff's interest in having the litigation in the forum (difficulty in bring suit elsewhere, availability of evidence, witnesses).

The interest of the interstate judicial system in obtaining the most efficient resolution to controversies and public policy.

Domestic corporations – a corporation is a resident of the forum if:

> 1) it is incorporated in the forum, or

> 2) it has its principal place of business in the forum.

Foreign corporations are subject to the jurisdictional requirements above.

Due process and federalism – the restriction on personal jurisdiction is the due process clause and its protection of individuals.

The sovereignty and rights of states outside the forum do not limit personal jurisdiction.

If federalism were an independent restriction, a defendant could never waive jurisdiction since individuals cannot waive states' rights.

Failure to comply with discovery orders aimed at a jurisdictional issue may be a waiver of jurisdiction.

Defamation – publication meets minimum contacts if the publisher avails itself of the market in a state (includes writers and editors).

Minimum contacts are evaluated in terms of specific or general jurisdiction.

Specific jurisdiction

The non-resident defendant has sufficient contacts with the forum, and those contacts are substantially related to the controversy (the cause of action arises out of the defendant's contact with the forum).

Injury within the forum alone is insufficient to establish jurisdiction over a non-resident defendant unless the defendant directed acts toward the forum and could reasonably expect to be hauled into court there (*World-Wide Volkswagen v. Woodson*, 1980).

All the defendant's contacts with the controversy do not have to be with the forum state so long as enough contacts are with the forum (*Burger King Corp. v. Rudzewicz,* 1985).

Merely placing a product into the stream of commerce may be insufficient unless the defendant has purposefully availed themself of the market (*Asahi Metals* – the court was fractured 4/4 on this issue; the unfairness of requiring the defendant to defend in California was determinative).

Brussels Convention – tort jurisdiction is at the place of acting or the location of the injury.

General jurisdiction

The non-resident defendant has extensive contacts with the forum justifying jurisdiction, and there are no contacts related to the controversy between the defendant and the forum.

The cause of action does not arise out of contact with the forum state.

Exercise of state court jurisdiction is discretionary based upon local court rules or statutes.

Suit not arising out of or related to the defendant's contacts with the forum state.

Sufficient contacts with the state amount to *continuous and systematic activity* in the state.

The minimum contacts threshold is significantly higher than the specific jurisdiction.

Individuals are subject to general jurisdiction in their domicile jurisdiction.

Continuous, systematic and substantial contact requirement

Helicopteros Nationales de Columbia v. Hall (1984) – purchasing equipment, using a bank for those purchases, and training pilots were insufficient forum activities to maintain a cause of action *arising out of* an accident in Columbia (court did not consider specific jurisdiction).

Brussels Convention – general jurisdiction exists only where a defendant is domiciled, incorporated, or has its corporate headquarters.

Piercing the corporate veil – asserting jurisdiction over a parent corporation requires a close relationship with the subsidiary (e.g., board of directors' overlap, direct involvement).

Alternatively, it requires misuse of the corporate identity.

Service of process is complete when served upon the subsidiary.

Partnerships – service on one partner or officer does not impute jurisdiction over property outside the state.

In rem jurisdiction

In rem: the subject of an action is some item of property ("*rem*") located in the forum and the action determines an interest in *rem* against the world:

> adjudicate questions concerning the ownership and control of the property (value of the judgment is limited to the "*rem*"),
>
> acts upon the thing itself rather than the rights of an individual (artificial distinction),
>
> minimum contacts established by the presence in the forum and notice.

Quasi in rem: The plaintiff asserts a preexisting interest in a dispute against specific named individuals only, and the judgment affects only those parties.

The value of the judgment cannot exceed the value of the "*rem*."

Land – a forum has jurisdiction over property located within the *situs*, and *in rem* judgments rendered will be subject to full faith and credit.

If a court only has *in rem* jurisdiction and issues a personal judgment (personal obligations), the judgment will be invalid.

Intangibles – the *situs* of an intangible determines jurisdiction.

A debtor's obligation accompanies them wherever they go and is subject to attachment provided there are minimum contacts.

Minimum contacts must be established to assert personal jurisdiction based upon attachment. The mere presence of unrelated property alone will not provide jurisdiction over persons (*Shaffer v. Heitner*, 1977 – shareholder derivative action failed minimum contacts).

Competence of the court

Subject matter jurisdiction refers to a court's power to hear and decide on an issue.

The parties cannot waive subject matter jurisdiction.

The court must address a lack of competence in its motion (even if parties do not challenge).

Parties cannot confer subject matter jurisdiction upon a court by agreement.

Full faith and credit does not apply to judgments rendered by courts that lack competence.

Continuing jurisdiction – once a court has jurisdiction over a defendant or their property, it retains that jurisdiction for proceedings which arise out of the original cause of action. Plaintiff may not add new claims without a jurisdictional basis. Irrelevant if the initial basis for jurisdiction no longer exists.

Domestic relations cases – a court may refuse to hear a case if the parties have moved elsewhere, and a convenient forum has jurisdiction over the defendant.

Obligation to provide or refuse a forum

A court must entertain a transitory cause of action that arises elsewhere

Refusal to hear a case because it arose under the law of a different state threatens interstate harmony (goal of full faith and credit).

The interests of the law-giving state should be considered unless the forum has substantive law to the contrary.

A forum is entitled to apply its statute of limitations to a transitory cause of action provided it is not discriminatory (state interest in not hearing stale claims).

Limits on the Exercise of Jurisdiction

Traditional limits for jurisdiction

Limitations imposed by contract – forum selection and consent to jurisdiction clauses

Prima facie valid and should be enforced unless unreasonable or unjust, procured by fraud, violative of public policy, or exceptionally inconvenient

Agreement denied effect when the parties and the incident were domestic, and the forum was a foreign country.

Clauses permit sophisticated parties to select the forum to resolve their disputes, and the courts show great deference to freedom of contracts in jurisdiction matters.

Bremen v. Zapata (offshore towing contract/forum selected) – influential factors included: international contract freely negotiated at arm's length, sophisticated parties, and the chosen forum was neutral.

Some courts have interpreted *Zapata* as creating a federal common law standard in diversity cases regardless of state standards.

Brussels' Convention – forum selection clauses vest exclusive jurisdiction in a member nation's court (one of the contracting parties must be from a member nation).

Fraud, force and privilege

A court will not exercise jurisdiction nor grant full faith and credit over a defendant or their property if the jurisdiction has been obtained by force or fraud.

Service of process achieved by tricking the defendant into entering the forum will be invalid.

Privilege – immunity from service applies to foreign sovereigns, defendant appearing specially, and a defendant who enters the forum to participate in civil litigation.

These limitations do not apply to a criminal defendant who will be subject to jurisdiction in the forum on civil matters once there.

Forum non conveniens

Forum non conveniens dismissal permits a court to refuse to exercise jurisdiction if it is an exceptionally inconvenient forum for the action, and a more convenient forum is available to the plaintiff.

Procedurally – motion is only available to the defendant.

The application depends upon the trial judge's sound discretion, who must consider the litigants' and the public's interests.

Litigant's interests – proximity and accessibility of evidence, availability of a compulsory process for unwilling witnesses, travel costs, ability to view the scene, and enforceability of a judgment.

Public interests – caseload pressures if litigation is shifted to popular forums, burden of jury duty, and the local interests of having cases decided where they arose.

The dismissal may be conditioned on submission to jurisdiction or waiver of the statute of limitations. However, it may not be conditioned on unilateral submission to U.S. discovery rules or supervision of a foreign action by a U.S. court.

A due process challenge against a foreign country judgment may be made when the plaintiff brings an enforcement action in a U.S. court.

An unfavorable change in the law is not grounds for the denial unless the remedy provided in the alternative forum is so inadequate that it is no remedy at all.

A presumption favoring the plaintiff's forum is more significant when the plaintiff is an American and the alternative forum is a foreign country.

Race to judgment – a defendant may initiate parallel litigation as a preemptive strike in a competent forum to prevent full faith and credit from binding him:

Most federal circuits follow the "first-filed rule" to decide which judgment has an effect.

State court or federal court with diversity jurisdiction – state law determines if the second forum action will be dismissed or stayed.

State injunction against parallel litigation – penalties available in the first state, but recognition and enforcement are not required in the second state.

Federal Transfer – for the convenience of the parties and witnesses, in the interests of justice, a district court may transfer a civil action to another district where it may have been brought.

A district court may not dismiss under *forum non conveniens* when there is an available district to transfer to

The district court has broader discretion to transfer than under a *forum non conveniens* dismissal.

Court where suit "may have been brought" refers to the defendant's ability and not the plaintiff's capacity (transferee court must have personal and subject matter jurisdiction).

The transferee district court must apply the state law of the transferor court (*Klaxon* rule).

Other jurisdictional limits imposed by the forum

2nd Restatement of Conflicts § 53 – a person will be ordered to act in another state when … required by the demands of justice and convenience. The defendant will not … be ordered to do an act that violates the law of another state.

A court can exercise its discretion and not require an action it has jurisdiction over if it will cause the party to violate the laws of a foreign forum.

It requires a balancing of interests.

Includes criminal laws, substantial sanctions equivalent to criminal penalties, or public policy as expressed in legislation.

Prospective civil liability is insufficient.

Foreign countries concerned with liberal U.S. discovery policy have enacted blocking statutes; however, a U.S. court with jurisdiction does not have to recognize such a statute.

Inability to grant relief – when relief is sought outside the framework of the local court system, the suit must be dismissed.

Slater v. Mexican National Railroad (1904) – the plaintiff was seeking a type of relief under Mexican law (revisable judgment for damages similar to a pension), which the local court was unable to grant.

Commerce clause – dismissal is mandatory when an action in a local court would impose an *unreasonable burden* on interstate commerce.

Statutes requiring general consent to jurisdiction before doing business in a state or consent to service by assignment of one ticket agent in a state are undue burdens on commerce.

The burden must be unreasonable since every transitory cause of action against a foreign corporation imposes some burden on trade.

Most of these cases can be decided on personal jurisdiction or *forum non conveniens* grounds without resort to the commerce clause.

A federal cause of action created by a constitutional act supersedes state law.

States cannot dismiss causes of action because the federal law is against the state's public policy (e.g., increases liabilities).

The principle applies when state and federal courts have concurrent jurisdiction.

Notes for active learning

Constitutional Limitations

Constitutional limitations for the jurisdiction of courts

The "Due Process" clause (5th and 14th Amendments) mandates that the exercise of personal jurisdiction meet the requirements of due process (*Pennoyer v. Neff,* 1878 – service by publication was ineffective for an action to determine the rights and obligations of parties).

Due process requires:

1) substantive due process (jurisdiction) – power over the person or property to assign liability, and

2) procedural due process (notice) – notice and an opportunity to be heard.

The state chosen must have significant contact with the parties or the subject matter of the litigation, which gives it a legitimate interest in seeing its law applied.

Courts do not have to weigh the interests, but if it meets the test.

Situations when the Pennoyer test is not met:

1) after the event in question, someone moves to a new state, and move creates only contact with that state; they cannot apply state law, or

2) if the only contact with the parties or the litigation is that the suit is brought in a state, they cannot apply state law.

Jurisdiction of courts for the choice of law

It is a violation of the due process clause for a forum to apply its law to the controversy when the only contact with the litigation is as the forum.

Home Insurance Co. v. Dick (1930) – the action involved an insurance contract on a tugboat where all the contacts were in Mexico, yet the Texas court applied its contract law (Supreme Court reversed).

If all contacts are with another state, the forum cannot constitutionally refuse to refer to foreign law.

If an actual conflict involves constitutional issues, it is ultimately for the Supreme Court to decide what is procedural and substantive, regardless of forum-applied labels.

The presumption that the law of the place of making determines the validity of a contract.

A forum must have enough contact with and interest in the dispute, so the application of its laws is neither arbitrary nor patently unfair.

De minimis contacts are not enough.

For example, in *Phillips Petroleum Co. v. Shutts* (1985), a small percentage of the plaintiff's gas leaseholds in the forum were insufficient for a nationwide class action.

Multi-state transactions – the forum will not be prevented from applying its law even though it conflicts with the other involved states provided it has a relationship to the action (e.g., injury to a domiciliary in the forum).

Foreseeability that an insured may end up in another justified state application of subsequent forum law to the contract.

Choice of Law

Choice-of-law concepts

Many cases are international or interstate:

The case has factual ties to two or more jurisdictions.

The case involves laws from two sources within the same jurisdiction.

Conflicts-of-law rules mitigate forum shopping and uphold the notions of fairness.

Principal courts decide what body of law to apply to a case; this determination of classification must be made following the law of the forum.

Courts faced with a choice-of-law issue generally have two choices:

1) a court can apply the law of the forum (*lex fori*) -- which is usually the result when the question of what law to apply is procedural, or

2) a court can apply the law of the site (*lex loci*) of the transaction or occurrence that gave rise to the litigation; usually, the controlling law selected when the matter is substantive.

Legal characterization of choice of law

Choice of law: choosing among competing legal principles by analyzing the law of applicable jurisdictions.

Vertical conflicts – conflicts between state and federal government.

Horizontal conflicts – conflicts between state governments.

2nd Restatement § 6: a court, subject to constitutional restrictions, will follow a statutory directive of its state on the choice of law.

If there is no such directive, the factors relevant to the choice of the applicable law include:

1) the needs of the interstate and international systems,

2) the relevant policies of the forum,

3) the applicable policies of other interested states and the relative interests of those states in the determination of the issue are the protection of justified expectations, the basic policies underlying the field of law to ensure certainty, predictability, and uniformity of result,

4) ease in the determination and application of the law to be applied.

Party autonomy to choose the applicable law

Fraternal organization internal affairs doctrine – the strong public policy of uniform application of laws governing a fraternal organization necessitates recognizing the law of the forum of incorporation.

Full faith and credit does not permit a state to legislate across state lines, and any state with a substantial interest in the matter can apply its law constitutionally.

Public acts are afforded full faith and credit, including statutes and case law of sister states.

2nd Restatement § 187 choice-of-law clauses

Struggles to reconcile the principle of party autonomy with the prerogative of the state to regulate contracts.

§ 187(2): issues parties could not have resolved by an explicit provision in their agreement, usually issues of contract validity (e.g., illegality, acceleration provisions, unenforceable based on forum law).

Limits on party autonomy – choice of laws is enforceable unless:

> state chosen must have a substantial relationship to the parties or the transaction, or

> there needs to be some other reasonable basis for selecting that state.,

> choice-of-law provisions are "unreasonable."

The fact that the choice of law would validate the contract is not enough of a reason.

Considerations include domicile, residence, nationality, place of incorporation, and place of business of the parties.

The forum state must have concern for the fundamental policy which the contractual choice of another state's law subverts.

The forum state must have a materially greater interest in the matter than the state whose law the parties have chosen.

Forum selection clauses

Forum selection clauses generally go with a choice-of-law clause and select the same jurisdiction.

§ 6 of Conflicts: the court will follow the directive of its state.

Without a directive, consider (not exclusive, and not listed in order of importance):

> needs of the interstate and international system,
>
> relevant policies of the forum,
>
> applicable policies of other interested states,
>
> justified expectations of the parties (not applied in tort cases)
>
> basic policies of law (the interested states' policies are essentially the same, but there are minor differences).

Courts apply local law to achieves underlying policies:

> certainty, predictability, and uniformity,
>
> discourage forum shopping,
>
> administrability.

Klaxon (1941) – federal district court in diversity must apply the choice-of-law rule of the state where it sits.

Van Dusen (1964) – transfer from a federal district court to another, the court to which case is assigned applies the law of the state from which it is transferred.

Notes for active learning

The Constitution and Choice of Law

Limits of legislative jurisdiction

The Constitution provides a baseline for rulings on due process or equal protection.

Constitutional protections for choice of law:

> reduce interstate friction,

> prevent unfair treatment to parties and promote individual fairness, or

> limit states' legislative ability.

Minimum contacts for due process is a more challenging test than for personal jurisdiction.

It does not dictate the choice of law unless the law of the state has insufficient contacts.

State interests and the constitution

Full faith and credit *vs.* due process (individual convergence) – the Supreme Court applies the following tests arbitrarily:

> due process,

> fairness prong (unfair surprise),

> *quid pro quo* (benefits and associated burdens),

> state interest must be legitimate as implicated in the facts of the case,

> minimum contacts,

> choice of law.

Obligation to provide a forum – if one state provides a cause of action, another state must provide a forum.

Full faith and credit clause overrides state laws that promote a state objective by preventing foreign action when the statute gives more deference to substantive rights.

Limitations on the rule:

> *forum non conveniens*,

> avoid burdens on forum courts,

> equal protection.

States may define substantive rights differently; if the forum has a legitimate interest (public policy conflict), it may apply its law.

Withholding from state courts the power to entertain claims based on the other states' laws is directly at odds with full faith and credit and must be subject to strict scrutiny and specific justification narrowly tailored to fit the rationale.

Renvoi and depecage

Renvoi (French for "send back" or "return unopened") is the principle of whether to apply the foreign state's "whole law" (including choice-of-law rules) or "internal law" (substantive).

This approach is generally rejected in the US except for questions of:

> title to land,
>
> questions concerning the validity of a decree of divorce, and
>
> settlement of estates.

Property entirely and exclusively within the sovereign of the state in which it is situated:

> estates can involve property in foreign countries,
>
> marital status be treated uniformly throughout the country,
>
> rights spring into existence in the jurisdiction where the property is located, so should use the property's locale for the choice-of-law rules.

Use renvoi whenever the objective of the choice-of-law rule is that the forum reaches the same result on the facts involved as would the courts of another state. It occurs when the other state has a dominant interest.

Remission – if renvoi is accepted and the state whose choice-of-law rules are examined refers the case back to the law of the forum state.

Partial remission – foreign choice of law refers to the internal law of the forum state.

1st Restatement – forum should ignore the foreign choice-of-law rules, except for the title of land and validity of a divorce decree, in which the whole law was accepted.

2nd Restatement – presumption that the choice of law refers to internal law unless uniformity considerations- unless it would trigger renvoi.

Depecage (French for "break into smaller pieces") is the treatment of an issue in a case by referring to the laws of more than one state (characterize or divide issues).

Under the vested rights approach, this dual reference was made to contract issues (e.g., place of making and performance).

Maryland Casualty Co. v. Jacek (1957) – the NJ court held that the issue of immunity was a tort issue and controlled by NY law, and the contract construction issue should be determined by NJ law (the place of the making).

By combining the law of the two states, the court frustrated the policy of each (prevention of collusion) without advancing the interests of either.

Depecage recognizes that a multi-state problem should not necessarily be decided the same way as a purely domestic case and can be used to accommodate the interests of several states.

Notice and proof of foreign law

Courts will take judicial notice of a sister-state and federal law.

The law of a foreign country is a fact, which must be pleaded and proved.

If foreign law cannot be determined, the resident state will apply the resident state law if there is no injustice.

The first response must tell the court what law should be applied.

Some courts assume laws are the same if not proven.

A court can take judicial notice of a sister state's law, but foreign law is unusual in this jurisdiction.

There are statutes authorizing courts to take judicial notice in pleadings or reasonable notice.

Foreign law must be pleaded like other facts, in conformity with the evidence, decided by a trier of fact, subject to only limited appellate review.

FRCP 44.1: the court may take judicial notice as a matter of law, therefore taking the decision of foreign law out of the jury's purview; limits review on appeal.

Notes for active learning

Choice-of-Law Theories

Traditional approaches to conflicts of law

Traditional theory uses a territorial approach (1st Restatement, Beale, vested rights); *lex loci* or law of the place.

History of conflicts of law – European common law historically used a territorial approach (Justice Story – 1st Restatement of Conflicts).

Currently, the interest of states has evolved from dissatisfaction with rigidity.

Vested rights approach (Beale) – localize events of multi-state, place in one state.

Pinpoints the jurisdiction where the parties' rights vest.

Law of the place uses where the last liable event occurred.

For contracts, the law of the location is of contracting.

For property, the law of the place where the property is located.

Party autonomy

Interpretation – intent of the parties determines the parties' expectations under the contract.

Validity affords an artificial device to encourage forum shopping.

For the intention to prevail, the choice of laws must be *bona fide* and in good faith.

The law chosen must have some relation to the agreement.

It cannot be contrary to evade U.S. policy.

No existence of a contrary statute.

2nd Restatement §187 – party autonomy may not be respected even if parties may not have been able to resolve by explicit provisions unless:

1) chosen law is contrary to the fundamental policy of the state, which has a materially more significant interest than the chosen state,

2) absent a contrary intent, reference is to the law of the chosen state.

Modern approaches to conflicts of law

The mere fact that a suit is brought in a state does not make it appropriate to apply the state's substantive law.

For a foreign suit, although the act complained of had no force in the forum, it gave rise to an obligation, which follows the person, and may be enforced where the person may be found.

Domestic rule of the foreign state when a forum case comes to the forum, it should apply its law but adopt and enforce as its law a rule of decision identical or highly similar to a rule of decision found in the law of the state.

UCC rule: a court must characterize issues to select the appropriate choice-of-law provision.

UCC rule: when a transaction bears a reasonable relation to this state and another state or notion, the parties may agree that the law of this state or the other governs the rights and duties; applies to transactions bearing a reasonable relation to the state.

Most significant relationship

Modern approach – 2nd Restatement uses the most significant relationship test.

Issues are separated, and the law of the state with the most significant relationship is applied.

The state as the center of gravity is the popular approach to conflicts because of manipulation, presumptions, and principles.

Judges favor it because of the enormous discretion given.

Interest analysis approach to choice of law

Babcock approach – list the factual contacts with the state.

Note the different state laws and find policies underlying each state law by consulting legislative history and court decisions.

Determine which state law would favor the plaintiff and which would favor the defendant.

Relate the facts to the policy to see if the state is interested in seeing its law applied.

The state has an interest if the party favored by a state's law resides in that state.

Apply the law of the state with the most significant governmental interest in the outcome.

Government interests analysis

General rule: the forum state's law applies unless the party requests another law to apply.

The forum should fundamentally follow its law through a series of steps.

First, the courts should look to policies expressed by the legislature in each jurisdiction.

If a party requests another law, identify the competing laws' policies by "the ordinary processes of construction and interpretation."

Identify the contacts of the parties considering the policies.

False conflicts: if only one state has an interest in having its law applied, the forum court should apply the law of the jurisdiction with interest in the outcome of the litigation.

True conflict: if two or more states are interested in the litigation, one of them is the forum state.

For true conflicts, the presumption is that the forum state's law applies unless the other state's interest is more significant.

If a conflict is unavoidable, the court should apply the law of the forum state.

Criticism challenges defining policy; courts can define policy to reach the desired results.

Allows for forum shopping because forum law is the default law applied to the case.

If the forum court is disinterested, but two or more states have legitimate competing interests, dismiss according to *forum non conveniens*.

Forum court uses its judgment on what law is appropriate or applies the law most closely resembling its own.

If no state has an interest, the court can dismiss the case or forum law governs.

Statutes directed to the choice of law

A court, subject to constitutional limitations, must follow the directions of its legislature.

The court must apply a local statutory provision directed to the choice of law if it would be constitutional to do so.

An example of a statute directed to the choice of law is the Uniform Commercial Code (UCC), which provides certain instances for applying the law chosen by the parties; in some other cases, apply the law of a particular state.

Another example is the Model Execution of Wills Act, which provides that the testator will subscribe to a written document shall be valid as to matters of the form if it complies with the local requirements of several enumerated states.

There are comparatively few statutes that expressly direct the choice of law.

Intended range of application of the statute

A court will rarely find that the statute explicitly covers a question of choice of law.

A court will rarely be directed by statute to apply the local law of one state rather than the local law of another in the decision of an issue.

The court questions whether the issue is within the intended range of the statute.

The court should give a local statute the range of application intended by the legislature when these intentions can be ascertained and constitutionally be given effect.

If the legislature intended that the statute be applied to the out-of-state facts involved, the court should apply it unless constitutional considerations forbid.

If the legislature intended that the statute be applied only to acts within the state, the statute should not be given a full range of applications.

Sometimes, a statute's intended range of application will be apparent on its face, as it expressly applies to citizens of a state, including those living abroad.

When the statute is silent about its range of application, the legislature's intent on the subject can sometimes be ascertained by the interpretation and construction.

Provided that it is constitutional to do so, the court will apply a local statute in the manner intended by the legislature even when another state's domestic law of another state would be applicable under general choice-of-law principles.

Rationale for choice of law

Legislatures usually legislate, and courts typically adjudicate for the locality.

Judges rarely consider the extent to which the laws they enact, and the common-law rules they enunciate, should apply to out-of-state facts.

When there are no adequate directives in the statute or the case law, the court considers the factors below determining the state whose local law will be applied to resolve the issue.

This list of factors is not exclusive, and a court considers other factors in deciding a question of choice of law.

It is not suggested that the factors mentioned are listed in order of their relative importance.

Varying weight will be given to factors in different areas for choice of law.

Favoring policies of the state with a dominant interest have predominant weight.

Transfers of interests in land are governed by the law the *situs*.

However, the policies in favor of protecting the parties' justified expectations and effectuating the basic policy underlying the field of law are essential.

Subject to certain limitations, the parties can choose the law to govern their contract and in the rules which provide, subject to certain restrictions or the validity of a contract against the charge of commercial usury.

The policy favoring uniformity of result gives rise to the rule that succession of interests in movables is governed by the law applied by the state courts where the decedent was domiciled at the time of their death.

Often, some of the factors point in different directions in all but the simplest case.

Hence any rule of choice of law, like other common-law rules, represents an accommodation of conflicting values.

2nd Restatement – the "most significant relationship."

Two-step process:

        start with an applicable presumptive rule,

        use § 6 with § 145 to determine which state has the most significant relationship.

§ 6 provides judges with a list of relevant factors (not an exclusive list):

        needs of the interstate and international systems,

        relevant policies of the forum,

        relevant policies of other interested states and the relative interests of those states in the determination of the issue,

        protection of justified expectations,

        basic policies underlying the field of law,

        certainty, predictability, and uniformity of result,

        ease in the determination and application of the law to be applied.

§ 145 highlights some contacts that matter:

> the place where the injury occurred,

> the place where the conduct causing the damage occurred,

> domicile, residence, nationality, place of incorporation and of business of the parties,

> place where the relationship, in any, between the parties, is centered.

Courts consider five principles that inform the forum's ultimate decision.

1) Predictability of results: respect what parties intended (e.g., contract cases).

2) Maintenance of interstate and international order: the forum should not "ruffle feather" by being too unseemly in the disregard of foreign law.

3) Simplification of the judicial task: often results concluding that the forum can apply forum or foreign law with equal ease (at least in domestic cases; foreign country law might be harder).

4) Advancement of the forum's governmental interests: what courts have done and what courts can be expected to do.

5) Application of the better rule of law (something more than different).

Statute of Limitations

Statutes of limitations and repose

Classic approach (*Wells v. Simonds Abrasive Co.*, 1953, Vinson): full faith and credit does not require applying another state's statute of limitations (SOL).

States are free to apply forum statute of limitations.

Not compelled to use the statute of limitations of the state whose substantive law applies.

Constitutional restraints (*Sun Oil v. Wortman*, 1988, Scalia): does not violate the full faith and credit to apply the longer local statute of limitations.

The Constitution is permissive as to applying the forum's substantive statute of limitations.

Choice-of-law approaches to limitations issues: states are free to make their own choice-of-law rules on limitations.

Borrowing statutes direct the forum to dismiss claims under foreign statutes of limitations in appropriate circumstances.

Tolling statutes suspend the running of the SOL against out-of-state defendants.

Uniform conflict of laws – limitation act

For claims substantively based upon the law of another state, the SOL of that state applies.

If a claim is substantively based upon the law of more than one state, the limitation period of one of those states chosen by the law of conflict of this state applies.

The limitation period of the forum state applies to all claims.

2nd Restatement § 142 statute of limitations

2nd Restatement §142 – the forum will apply its statute of limitations barring a claim unless exceptional circumstances of the case make such results unreasonable.

The forum applies its SOL barring the claim if the forum's statute of limitations is shorter.

A state will not give longer life to a cause of action arising in another state than its own.

The forum applies its SOL permitting the claim if the forum's SOL is longer, unless:

1) maintain the suit would serve no substantial interest in the forum, and

2) a suit would be barred under the statute of limitations of a state having a more significant relationship to the parties and occurrence.

Borrowing statutes: if action accrued elsewhere, cannot use forum's statute of limitations.

Tolling rules and statute of limitations

Savings statutes preserve a cause of action that would usually be barred (e.g., file in district court on diversity), the statute of limitations tolls, and no subject matter jurisdiction. The plaintiff can refile in the state for one year after dismissal.

Statute of repose: suit barred from the date of some specific event.

Etheridge v. Genie Industries, Inc., Ala. (1994): statutes of repose are procedural unless they are inextricably bound in a statute creating the right or cause of action.

Because the statute of repose existed in a different section than the cause of action and contained a list of other causes of action to which it applied, the statute was not sufficiently connected to the cause of action; therefore, not substantive.

Application in Specific Areas

Choice of laws for specific areas

The traditional system for choice of law was based on the vested rights theory in the 1st Restatement of Conflicts.

Vested rights – the forum is to apply the law of the state in which the rights of the parties vest (where they are created).

The forum must first characterize the cause of action (e.g., torts, contracts, property).

Approximately one-third of the states still use traditional rules.

Under the 1st Restatement, the forum does not consider the scope or policy of the substantive rule of law until after the state is chosen.

Torts – law of the place where the accident occurred.

1st Restatement § 378: the law of the place of the wrong determines if there is a legal injury.

The instant the cause of action (COA) arises, the plaintiff's rights vest.

Apply the law of the place where the injury or place of wrong occurred.

This may not be the place of negligence (or other wrongs) but the place of injury.

Place of wrong – use the law of the state of consequences, not original wrong / negligence where the force impinged on the plaintiff's body.

Each state has legislative jurisdiction to determine the legal effects of acts done or events caused within a territory.

Laws of the state are intended to possess exclusive sovereignty and jurisdiction within its territory, and persons who are residents and contracts made and acts done within it:

> compensate the plaintiff for the harm they suffered,
>
> provide predictability protecting reasonable expectations of the parties,
>
> provide uniformity and administrability,
>
> discourage forum shopping.

Where harm is done to the person's reputation, the place of wrong is where the defamatory statement was communicated.

Invasion of privacy uses the law of the jurisdiction where the plaintiff was when their feelings were wounded.

Exceptions to the place of the wrong test:

1) if the wrong depends on the application of the standard of care, that standard should be taken from the law of the location of the actor's conduct;

2) a person required, forbidden, or privileged to act under the law of the "place of acting" should not be held liable for consequences on another state.

Problems with the territorial approach:

determine where the injury occurred by looking at the localizing event (e.g., reputation, trademark, mass tort case),

unfairness potential,

characterization or escape devices,

renvoi.

Rights under a contract vest at the moment the contract is made.

Apply the law of the place of the making of the contract.

Clear rules but may lead to a state with no policy interest in the outcome of the litigation.

American rule: the place of contract for specific issues (e.g., validity, capacity).

The place of contract determines capacity.

Place of performance for other issues

Old law: the law only if there is a connection.

If a contract is completed in another state, it makes no difference whether the person goes in person, sends an agent, or writes a letter across the boundary lines between the states.

English rule: parties' intent, if unclear, is the "closest and most real connection."

Rome Convention eliminated "mandatory rules," replacing them with "overriding mandatory provisions."

Party autonomy – parties may choose but be limited by "mandatory rules" of the country where the contract was made.

A court can apply its law if it considers the law "overriding," providing much discretion.

Default rule (absent choice) § 4 – "most closely connected."

Presumption (closest connection) § 4(2) – "characteristic performance."

A contract's validity is to be decided by the law of the place where the contract is made unless it is to be performed in another country.

If the contract is to be performed in another place as intended by the parties, the validity, nature, obligation, and interpretation are governed by the location of performance.

Freedom of contract dominates in most states, with some restrictions (2nd Restatement).

Juenger – parties should be free to select their own rules that reflect commercial practice and the best law without regard for the desires of sovereigns.

Place of contracting

Special rules determine where the contract is made depending on the type of conflict.

§311 Place of contracting: principal event necessary to make a contract occurs.

§312 Formal contract: effective on delivery, place of contracting is where delivery is made.

§323 Informal unilateral contract: where the event takes place that makes it binding.

§325 Informal bilateral contract: where the second promise is made in consideration of the first promise.

§326 Acceptance from one state to another: if acceptance is sent by an agent of the acceptor, the state where the agent delivers it or from which acceptance is sent.

§332 Validity and effect of the contract: the law of the place where the contract was made (capacity, necessary form, consideration, requirements to make a promise binding, time, and place where the promise is to be performed, the character of the promise).

§358: performance handled with the place where a contract is to be performed (i.e., manner, time, locality, parties involved, sufficiency, an excuse for non-performance).

Justifiable expectations of parties are enforceable.

Property

Law of *situs* – the place of the property is to govern as to the capacity of the testator. Also determines marriage, property, mortgages, etc.

Immovables are of the most considerable concern: exclusive jurisdiction to the state in which they are situated.

Leaseholds are considered immovable.

Pragmatic concerns – recording system for land interests.

Movables – the law of the *situs* does not always apply as there are many exceptions.

Situs is determined at the time of possession.

Location during litigation to avoid forum shopping.

For distribution between spouses, apply the place of marital domicile.

The Restatement for the choice-of-law issues states the rules in which the courts have evolved in accommodation with specific factors.

For property, such rules are sufficiently precise to permit them to be applied in the decision of a case without explicit reference to the factors which underlie them.

Wills and intestate succession

For land, the law of the *situs* applies.

Movable property – law of the *situs,* but issues arise (e.g., the *situs* of stock certificate).

Personal property – the domicile of the decedent at death.

The policy governs the status of property *vs.* determining who takes under a will (*situs* rule fractionalizes estate but might be consistent with expectations).

For wills, it might be better to look at domicile at the time of execution.

Intestate succession is determined by domicile. Domicile is determined by the law of the forum and requires physical presence and intent to remain indefinitely.

Modern rule – domicile depends on the issue (old rule: unitary).

White v. Tennant (WV 1888) (moved from PA to WV but for less than one day): domicile was established upon arrival.

Estate of Jones (Iowa 1921) (Lusitania): death in transit uses the previous domicile until "new domicile is secured."

Family law

Marriage is valid where the wedding was celebrated or performed.

Exception: marriage would violate the state's public policy; then, it may not be recognized even though it was valid where performed.

Marriages void where performed are void everywhere.

Exception: if marriage is void because of failure to comply with the technical requirement of the state where it is performed, it can still be recognized in the resident state if it would have complied with the resident state rule.

Wilkins v. Zelichowski (NJ 1959); NJ statute for marriage by an underage woman is void if not confirmed. The statute demonstrated "strong public policy" against recognizing marriages of minor women in other states.

2nd Restatement: most significant relationship to spouses and marriage (usually the place of celebration unless it violates another state's policy with the most significant relationship).

Divorce is governed by the law of the plaintiff's domicile.

Domicile (judicial construction, as opposed to the residence) is a legislative term usually meaning without intent to stay.

A person has one domicile and only one domicile.

Domicile requires the coexistence of physical presence and intent to remain.

A person may not have enough relationship with their domicile unless they have been there for a significant time.

In the modern approach, domicile shifts depending on the burden (i.e., taxes *vs.* intestate succession). If there is a rupture in marital relations, one spouse may acquire their domicile even if they are the party at fault.

1st Restatement said that a spouse could not change their domicile without going there first, but 2nd Restatement provides that the other spouse's presence may serve as a substitute.

If a home straddles the border, it could be the principal entrance or where the person sleeps.

A person cannot (1st Restatement) or does not usually (2nd Restatement) acquire a domicile by the presence in a place under physical or legal compulsion.

1st Restatement: marriage is valid everywhere if legal in the state where celebrated.

Notes for active learning

Additional principles for application in specific areas

Torts – *lex loci delicti commissi* [Latin, *the law of the place where the tort was committed*] controls.

Lex loci [Latin, *the law of the place*] applies even though the significant contacts, including the negligent act, occurred in another state.

Vicarious liability is determined by the place of the wrong only if the defendant authorized the tortfeasor to act for them in the state.

Lex loci determines the character and measure of the damages, the standard of care, causation, contributory negligence, master-servant rule, defenses, and survival of actions.

Contracts – *lex loci contractus* (*"law of the place where the contract is made"*) applies.

Issues concerning performance are governed by the law of the place of performance.

The forum decides where the contract was made.

The state whose law is applied to the dispute may have no interests at stake (other than being the place of contracting).

Where the contract is made is subject to interpretation based upon the nature of the modern commercial transaction.

The issue may be characterized as one of performance to apply different laws and achieve the desired result. In *Louis-Dreyfus v. Paterson Steamships, Ltd* (1930), each state favored limiting liability, but the *lex loci* rule did not. To advance the interests of the involved states, the court characterized the dispute as performance.

Contracts – party expectations may determine the choice of law.

A court may ignore the *lex loci* law and apply the law of the place of performance to resolve a contract dispute if it determines that the parties entered into their obligation because of that law (contract is invalid under *lex loci* law but enforceable in place of performance)

An adhesion contract (steamship ticket) may designate the law to be applied regardless of *lex loci* if the forum selected has some connection to the agreement.

Usury – courts tend to apply whichever law upholds the validity of the contract if there is a reasonable relationship to the transaction and the parties were in equal bargaining positions.

2nd Restatement § 203 usury – a contract is enforceable if its interest rate is permitted in a state with a substantial relationship to the contract and does not significantly exceed the price allowed by an interested state.

The presumption of validity is necessary to promote the free flow of commerce; otherwise, lenders may be reluctant to lend money.

For real property, the law of the *situs* determines the disposition and succession of real property. This is necessary to administer and ensure the accuracy of title records.

Only courts of the *situs* can directly affect title to land in that state because states have a strong interest in the property within their borders.

Hague Convention and Civil Law countries use law of the possessor's domicile and not *situs*.

Forum law is traditionally applied to domestic, workman's compensation, and criminal matters regardless of the choice-of-law rules.

Applying choice-of-law rules to specific issues

For contracts, the difficulties and complexities involved have prevented the courts from formulating precise rules, which provide satisfactory accommodation of the underlying factors in situations that may arise.

Courts state the general principle, such as applying the local law "of the state of the most significant relationship," to provide perspective about the correct approach but this approach does not furnish precise answers.

The courts must look at the underlying factors to arrive at a decision.

A statement of precise rules in choice of law is complicated by the variety of facts and issues.

Many of these issues have not been thoroughly explored by the courts. These rules represent general statements frequently used by the courts in opinions and the rationale of the decisions in more recent opinions.

Substance *vs.* procedure

Forum determines whether procedural rules or substantive law applies.

Pros of applying forum law (i.e., characterizing as procedural):

> administrative convenience,
>
> courts would have to read pleadings for substance (e.g., determining deadlines),
>
> administration of justice (e.g., rules of evidence),
>
> advance policy, but focus on adjudication, not determining the rights of parties,
>
> courts apply their evidence rules for judicial efficiency.

1ˢᵗ Restatement (§ 390) – when foreign law is applicable, it governs the substantive law; the laws of the forum govern the procedure.

The court of the forum decides the procedure.

The assumption is that the rule will be manipulated. It offers little or no guidance on why one type of characterization is better.

Criteria for distinguishing:

> characterization in statute or precedent,

> outcome determinative.

The remedy is procedural, and the right is substantive.

The court of the forum applies the rules of a foreign system until it becomes inconvenient.

Needs of the interstate and international systems

The function of choice-of-law rules is to make interstate and international systems work well.

Choice-of-law rules should seek to further harmonious relations between states and facilitate commercial intercourse.

In formulating rules of choice of law, a state should regard the needs and policies of other states and the community of states.

Choice-of-law rules for policy are likely to commend other states and be adopted by them.

Adopting the same choice-of-law rules by many states furthers the needs of the interstate and international systems and the values of certainty, predictability, and uniformity of results.

Relevant policies of the state of the forum

Two situations should be distinguished.

> The state of the forum has no interest in the case apart from the fact that it tries the action. The relevant policies of the state of the forum will be embodied in its rules relating to trial administration.

> The state of the forum has an interest in the case apart from the fact that it is the place of trial. The relevant policies of the forum state may be embodied in rules that do not relate only to trial administration.

Whether embodied in a statute or a common-law rule, every rule of law was designed to achieve a purpose.

A court should consider these purposes in determining whether to apply its rule or the rule of another state in deciding the issue.

If the purposes sought to be achieved by a local statute or its application to out-of-state facts furthers the common-law rule, this is a weighty reason for such a claim.

The court is under no compulsion to apply the statute or rule to such out-of-state facts since the originating legislature or court had no ascertainable intent on the subject.

The court must decide whether the purposes sought to be achieved by a local statute or rule should be furthered at the expense of the other choice-of-law factors mentioned.

Relevant policies of other interested states

In determining a question of choice of law, the forum should consider its relevant policies and the applicable policies of the interested states.

The forum should seek to reach a result achieving the best accommodation of these policies.

The forum should appraise the relative interests of the states involved in the determination of the issue.

In general, the state with interests most deeply affected should have its local law applied.

The state of dominant interest may depend upon the issue involved.

If a person injures their spouse in a state other than that of their domicile, it may be that the state of conduct and injury has the dominant interest in determining whether the conduct was tortious or whether the injured spouse was guilty of contributory negligence.

The spouse's domicile state is the state of dominant interest regarding whether the person who caused the injury should be held immune from tort liability to their spouse.

The relevant local law rule may determine whether this state has the dominant interest.

For example, applying a state's statute or common-law rule, which absolves the defendant from liability, could not be justified based on this state's interest in the welfare of the injured plaintiff.

Protection of justified expectations

The justified expectation is an essential value in law, including the choice of law.

It would be unfair and improper to hold a person liable under the local law of one state when they had justifiably comported conduct to conform to the requirements of another state.

Partly because of this factor, the parties are free within broad limits to choose the law to govern the validity of their contract and that the courts seek to apply a law that will sustain the validity of a trust of movables.

There are occasions, particularly in negligence, when the parties act without giving thought to the legal consequences of their conduct or to the law that may be applied.

In such situations, the parties have no justified expectations to protect and are not factored into the decision of a choice-of-law question.

Basic policies underlying the field of law

Basic policies underlying jurisprudence are important when the policies of the interested states are mostly the same, but there are minor differences between relevant local rules.

In such instances, there is a good reason for the court to apply the local law of that state, which achieves the policies underlying jurisprudence.

For example, courts seek to apply laws that sustain the validity of a contract against the charge of commercial usury or the validity of a trust of movables against the charge of violating the rule against perpetuities.

Predictability and uniformity of result

Predictability and uniformity are essential values in law.

To the extent that they are attained in choice of law, forum shopping will be discouraged.

These values can, however, be purchased at too high a price.

In a rapidly developing area, such as the choice of law, it is often more important than ethical rules developed for predictability, and uniformity of result should be assured through continued adherence to existing rules.

Predictability and uniformity of results are essential in areas where the parties are likely to preemptively consider the legal consequences of their transactions.

Parties are permitted within broad limits to choose the law that will determine the validity and effect of their contract.

The law applied by the courts of the state of the *situs* determines the validity of transfers of interests in land.

Uniformity of result is important when transferring an aggregate of movables situated in different states.

The law applied by the courts of the state of a decedent's domicile at death determines the validity of their will for movables and the distribution of movables in the event of intestacy.

While courts consider the ease of determining and applying the law, it is not overemphasized since producing predictable and uniform results is of greater importance.

The policy does provide a goal for which to strive.

Reciprocity

In formulating common-law rules of choice of law, the courts are rarely guided by reciprocity considerations.

Private parties should not suffer from the courts of the state from which they consider the interests of the state of the forum.

The satisfactory development of choice-of-law rules can best be attained if each court considers other states' interests without regard to whether the courts of one or more of these other states would do the same. For example, whether reciprocity is a condition to recognize and enforce a judgment of a foreign nation.

States sometimes incorporate a principle of reciprocity into statutes and treaties.

They may do so to induce other states to take specific actions favorable to their interests or the interests of their citizens.

Many states have enacted statutes that provide that a suit by a sister state for the recovery of taxes will be entertained in the local courts if the sister state courts would consider a similar lawsuit by the state of the forum.

Additionally, some states provide by statute that an alien cannot inherit local assets unless their citizens, in turn, would be permitted to inherit in the state of the alien's nationality.

A principle of reciprocity is sometimes employed in statutes to permit reciprocating states to obtain by cooperative efforts what a single state could not achieve through the force of its law.

Federal courts applying state law

Federal courts apply different rules than state courts because federal jurisdiction is limited to what has been enumerated in the Constitution.

In a case based on diversity of citizenship, a federal court determines the conflict-of-law issue as if it were the highest court in the state in which it is sitting.

The rules that federal courts must obey regarding which laws to apply are complex.

Federal courts apply choice-of-law rules instead of the law of the forum to discourage forum shopping. This could result in courts applying their law to cases with no connection to the forum.

Parties have expectations about how and which law governs.

Notes for active learning

Defenses Against Application of Foreign Law

Escape mechanisms to forego applying a state's law

Exception for other transactions (2nd Restatement): allow the choice-of-law clause unless the chosen state has no substantial relationship with the parties or transaction and no other reasonable basis for the parties' choice.

A court can apply a law that has a materially more significant interest in the dispute.

Choice-of-forum clauses designate the court where the dispute will be resolved.

Parties can agree that the litigation should be conducted in another forum but must be reasonable at the time of litigation.

Substance *vs.* procedure:

> procedure rules govern the conduct of litigation,

> substance rules govern out-of-court conduct,

> procedural law applies to the forum state.

Characterization

When characterizing a hybrid transaction (e.g., a land sale contract), characterize it as a "property" case to get the *situs* rule.

Examiners prefer the *situs* rule due to the statute of limitations and borrowing statutes.

A court should apply the shorter of two competing statutes of limitations.

Public policy

Courts refuse to apply foreign law if it is contrary to a strong public policy in the forum state.

A court must carefully consider the decision concerning public policy.

Public policy is a part of the conflict of laws, difficult to reconcile with vested rights.

It must be a dramatic departure from the court's idea of justice or fairness.

1st Restatement § 612 precludes suits upon a cause of action created in another state, the enforcement of which is contrary to the forum's public policy.

The court should look to determine public policy based upon legislative debates, constitution, and public opinion.

Application of public policy exception: penal and tax laws of another jurisdiction will not be enforced, as they are intimate notions of another state's identity.

Penal laws award a penalty to the state, public officer, or member of the public suing in the community interest to address a public wrong.

Criminal law does not include wrongful death or corporate director's misconduct because they satisfy a pre-existing claim of right.

Applying state law in diversity cases

A federal court must apply the state's choice-of-law rules in which it sits; *Klaxon Co. v. Stentor Mfg. Co.* (1941).

Courts prefer uniform administration, although Congress is not constitutionally barred from creating federal choice-of-law rules.

Forum non conveniens avoids state conflict-of-laws issues.

Private interest factors include sources of proof, witnesses, practical problems with ease of trial (e.g., impleading third parties).

Public interest factors include a jury's duty with deciding a case, local interest in dealing with the matter, a judge's familiarity with local law, and the interest of the state.

The effect of transfer

§ 1404 permits transfer within federal courts instead of dismissal but uses the same though less rigid factors in deciding transfer.

§ 1404(a) is the codification of *forum non conveniens*: exists when a federal court cannot transfer to the better forum (foreign or state court).

Under §1404(a) (*forum non conveniens*): the transferee court will apply the law of the transferor court (*Van Dusen v. Barrack,* 1964). Use the same factors as *forum non conveniens* in deciding to transfer. It is meant as a transfer of courts for convenience, not for law.

Proper enforcement of the forum selection clause is through § 1404(a) and not § 1406(a).

Van Dusen rule (the choice of law should be that of the state where the case was filed initially) does not apply because it cannot ignore the agreed-to forum's law.

Gulf Oil (1947) analysis changes:

>plaintiff's choice merits no weight because they agreed to the forum by contract,
>
>no private interest factors because already decided based on contract,
>
>may consider argument about public-interest factors only.

Constitutional Constraints on Choice of Law

Judicial discretion

The courts can generally apply whatever law they see fit so long as their choice is neither arbitrary nor fundamentally unfair.

Two constitutional provisions limit a court's ability to apply choice of laws if:

> there are no plausible or cognizable connections, or

> a party could not reasonably have anticipated the application of forum law.

Due process (14th Amendment) – application of a law is so unconnected to a party it could deprive that party of property without due process.

Full faith and credit (4th Amendment) goes beyond respecting judgments; states must recognize the acts of other states.

Early cases trended towards constitutionalizing choice-of-law principles.

Application of forum law where the forum has no connections or minimal connections to the dispute violates due process (*Home Insurance Co. v. Dick,* 1930, Brandeis) is still good law.

Rights created by contract in the state must use contracting state's law or violates full faith and credit (*Bradford Electric Light Co. v. Clapper*, 1932, Brandeis).

Analysis of full faith and credit and due process seem to have merged; no distinction between the two for determining the constitutionality of choice-of-law rule application.

Choosing forum law

Choosing forum law when other state does not have a significantly greater interest than the forum does not violate full faith and credit (*Alaska Packers Ass'n v. Industrial Accident Commission,* 1935, Stone).

Prima facie – every state is entitled to enforce in its courts its statutes, lawfully enacted.

Full faith and credit clause does not require the forum state to apply the other state's law when the policies of two states conflict in the form of conflicting statutes, and the interest of the non-forum state is not superior to that of the forum state.

It is constitutionally sufficient that the forum has a plausible or cognizable interest in applying its law to the dispute (*Pacific Employers Ins. Co. v. Industrial Accident Board*, 1939).

Like *Alaska Packers*, the court provides no substantive look at another state's interest; because it has an interest, it is constitutional to apply its law.

Applications of minimal scrutiny

The choice of law only offends the 14th Amendment if the state has no significant contact or significant aggregation of conduct with the parties, transaction, or occurrence (*Allstate Ins. v. Hague*, 1981, Brennan). Constitutional to apply MN law because MN has enough contacts.

No contact violates the Constitution (*Phillips Petroleum Co. v. Shutts*, 1985, Rehnquist).

Unconstitutional for KS courts to apply KS law to claims with which KS had no significant contacts – would be arbitrary and unfair (full faith and credit).

Federal–State Conflicts

Erie doctrine

Federal courts with diversity jurisdiction apply the law of the state in which they sit.

Federal courts have no authority to apply rules of law drawn from some amorphous body of "general law."

Unconstitutional because federal courts have no delegated power to declare substantive laws.

Reasoning – prior law (*Swift*) prevented uniformity; impossible to determine general law *vs.* local law.

Erie R.R. Co. v. Tompkins (1938) interpreted the Federal Rules of Decision Act to require federal courts, in diversity actions, to apply state statutory and common law to substantive issues when there is no federal statute on point and federal law is procedural.

After *Erie*, federal courts in diversity follow the state supreme court predictive approach; predict how the state's highest court would rule if it heard the case.

The Rules of Decision Act 28 U.S.C. § 1652 states that in civil actions, the federal courts must apply the "law of the several states, except where the Constitution, or treaties of the U.S., or acts of Congress otherwise require or provide."

Under the Rules of Decision Act, the Constitution, treaties, and constitutional acts of congress always take precedence, where relevant, over state provisions; applies to proceedings in state and federal court.

In the absence of a controlling federal provision, the federal courts will be bound to follow state constitutions, statutes, and common law in a diversity action.

"Substantive" versus "Procedural" test – matters characterized as substantive would be governed by state law while procedural matters (concern the process by which the claims of rights are examined) would be governed by federal law.

The Supreme Court rejected the concept of federal common law in diversity actions.

Federal common law survives in matters which are exclusively within the purview of the federal courts such as Admiralty, Maritime, etc. (lawmaking power has not been granted to the states by the constitution, and there has been no congressional action to the contrary), in which case, it is controlling because of the supremacy clause of the Constitution.

The court applied the following rationale in invoking the Erie doctrine:

Uniformity of law sought under *Swift v. Tyson* never materialized and yielded inequitable administration of the law. Non-citizens gained a forum shopping advantage, which allowed them to evade potentially unfavorable state common-law rules (*Black & White Taxicab,* 1928 re-incorporated in another state for diversity and avoid an adverse decision in state court).

Sovereignty – the authority of the states to regulate their affairs was eroded by *Swift v. Tyson.*

Ascertaining the state law

Klaxon doctrine requires the federal court to apply the conflict-of-law rules of the state where the federal court sits.

Conflicts of law arise when the federal court is sitting in one state, and the cause of action arose in another, each with different laws.

When a case is transferred under § 1404 to another federal district court, the transferee court must apply the transferor court's substantive law and its conflict-of-law rules:

> state constitutions or statutes are determinative, or

> holdings on point by the highest court in the state.

When there is no holding on point, the federal court must decide what the state's highest court would do if confronted with the same issue.

Certification: some states permit, by statute, questions of law to be "certified" to the highest court in the state for a determination.

Some states allow courts to decide issues in controversy before them, considering:

> time allocation,

> abstract question removed from the case.

Abstention: a federal court can suspend its inquiry and require a plaintiff to bring the case in state court first if:

> the state law is unsettled, and

> interpretation will have serious public policy implications for the state.

Therefore, some states will not certify a case initially brought in federal court.

Limitation of state power in federal courts

The *Outcome Determinative test* (*Guaranty Trust Co. v. York*, 1945 – SC applied the NY statute of limitations rather than the federal so as not to bar litigation).

State rules control if the choice between state or federal requirements could be outcome determinative in the case.

Rationale: the result of a diversity case in a federal court should be substantially the same (so far as legal rules determine the outcome) as it would be in state court.

Contrasting substance and procedure is inadequate; any matter outcome-determinative would be substantive. The dilemma is that procedural matters can be outcome determinative.

When considering outcome determination, evaluate the rationale under *Erie*:

> 1) avoidance of inequitable administration of the law, and

> 2) prevention of forum shopping.

Statute of limitations is outcome determinative for *Erie* purposes.

The *Balancing test* (*Byrd v. Blue Ridge Rural Electric Cooperative, Inc.*) – the court applied a balancing test between the competing federal and state interests advanced by their respective procedural rules. The court held that the federal interest of a jury trial under the 7th Amendment was an overriding interest when compared to the state's workman's compensation regulations. The court considered:

> state rights and obligations,

> disruption to the federal system of distribution of functions,

> outcome determinative.

The *Modified Outcome Determinative test* effectively builds a protective wall around the Federal Rules of Civil Procedure and removes them from the scope of the *Erie* doctrine.

In *Hanna v. Plumer* (1965), the court held in favor of service of process under the federal rules, which conflicted with service under state law.

Federal Rules of Civil Procedure supersede state procedure

The Rules arise under the Rules Enabling Act and thus supersede state procedural law they conflict with (supremacy clause).

A conflict may be the result of:

> 1) a direct collision between a federal rule and a state law, or

> 2) the federal rule may "occupy the same field" as the state law.

The Rules supersede conflicting state laws whenever they are on point and constitutional.

If there is no conflict, both federal and state rules may be applied.

A Rule is constitutional if it arises under the Rules Enabling Act and is rationally capable of being classified as procedural. If a federal rule arises under the Enabling Act, is on point, and is constitutional, it is binding.

A Rule may only be invalidated if the advisory committee, Supreme Court or Congress erred in promulgating it. No Federal Rule has been found invalid under the Act.

If a Rule is on point and conflicts with state law, the Rule supersedes.

Application of federal rules

Hanna does not overrule *Byrd* since references to *Erie* are only *dicta*.

Pure *Erie* cases (arising under the Rules of Decision Act) require the application of the outcome determinative or balancing test considering the rationale behind the *Erie* doctrine:

> forum shopping, and

> inequitable application of the law.

Privileges – under Rule 501, state-created privileges are substantive and outcome-determinative, there is no federal interest, and state policy should not be thwarted by diversity.

Walker v. Armco Steel (1980) – Rule 3, which provides that the filing of the complaint commences a civil action, does not affect the tolling of the statute of limitations.

The purpose of Rule 3 is to offer time parameters for federal procedural requirements (e.g., filing an answer); thus, there is no conflict between Rule 3 and the state statute of limitations.

Cases may turn on a narrow interpretation of the Rule. If a Rule is interpreted more broadly, it supplants state law.

Federal questions concerning state law

Congress may specify the Rule of Decision to be applied, superseding contrary state rules.

Federal courts have developed a specialized common law to decide cases where:

> the subject matter must be governed by federal law,

> there are no congressional enactments,

> the issue is within federal law-making competence and not addressed by Congress,

> there are vital federal interests and the necessity of a uniform national standard (federal interests may be inferred from related statutes).

If federal common law applies, there is no *Erie* problem because of the Supremacy Clause.

If Congress subsequently addresses the issue, the statute supersedes the earlier federal common-law rule.

A case based on federal common law is a "federal question," and a state court hearing a claim must apply the federal rule.

Similarly, a federal court sitting in diversity must apply the federal common law.

This rule applies to claims where the underlying basis of the action lies within the federal common law's scope. For example, a lawyer sues a defendant for inducing their client to fire them in a maritime case. This tort action is subject to federal common law since there is a need for uniformity in maritime affairs.

Federal law governs questions involving the rights of the U.S. arising under nationwide federal programs.

The rights and duties of the U.S. on commercial paper are included. State law governs disputes between private parties regarding commercial paper (e.g., conversion of U.S. bonds).

State law may be incorporated if there is little need for a special federal rule for uniformity. This is especially applicable in commercial transactions since states have adopted the UCC, and parties enter such transactions relying on state law.

International conflicts and foreign affairs

Foreign relations are within the authority of the executive branch of the federal government, and judicial interference is likely to frustrate national goals.

Act of state doctrine precludes the courts from questioning the validity of the actions of a foreign sovereign effective within its territory.

Foreign affairs are governed by federal law only (even if a state has enacted the doctrine in terms identical to federal decisions).

The doctrine has its underpinnings in comity and the constitutional separation of powers.

The doctrine only applies where the court would have to determine the validity of foreign government actions (mere embarrassment of the foreign government is insufficient).

District courts typically define the question as jurisdictional or as a choice-of-law problem.

Actions of foreign governments fall within the doctrine if:

>taking of property (could be other action),

>occurs within the sovereign's territory,

>sovereignty is recognized at the time of the suit,

>there is no treaty or additional unambiguous agreement on the subject.

A state cannot condition conveyance of real property to citizens of a foreign country upon a reciprocal right to American citizens since such a law intrudes upon foreign affairs.

A state law that is neutral on its face may result in a different outcome.

State action in the field may infringe on federal authority, or it may be meaningless since it has no effect.

State statutes prohibiting state pension fund investment in companies doing business in certain countries may prevail since the state is a market participant. However, some lower court have struck down such a statute.

Any party may invoke the act of state doctrine, but only a foreign sovereign can raise the defense of sovereign immunity (governed by statute).

For insurance policies, courts perform interest analysis (e.g., the grouping of contacts) to determine which law applies (basically a private matter). Courts generally apply the law of the insured risk to genuine conflicts.

Monetary conversion is determined as of the judgment date (e.g., NY rule).

Avoidance of doctrine – characterization of the action or nature of the law involved.

Cases with international scope apply the same choice-of-law rules as in interstate settings.

Foreign sovereign compulsion does not create a conflict of law issue; instead, it is a defense.

Legislative jurisdiction (jurisdiction to prescribe) is a consideration in international cases.

Treaties with foreign nations supersede local laws.

Recurring Problems of Conflict of Laws

Federalism for choice of laws

Erie doctrine: no federal common law (not bound by statute) in diversity cases, apply the substantive law (statutes and precedent) of the state where a court sits.

Erie doctrine does not apply in federal questions, except as governed by statutes or the Constitution.

There is no federal general common law; case law (judge-made law) delegates lawmaking authority to judges.

Federal common law exists by judges filling in the gaps (e.g., the Sherman Antitrust Act, Alien Tort Claims Act).

Implications on the choice of laws:

> *Klaxon* (1941) – federal court sitting in diversity does have to apply the choice-of-law regime of the state where they are sitting;
>
> *Swift v. Tyson* (1842) – common law contract case;
>
> Rules of Decision Act (1948) – a federal court applies the law of the state where no federal law exists (does not apply to judge-made law);
>
> Federal courts sitting in diversity need not apply the state's unwritten law, can develop common law interpretation.

Disadvantages

Forum shopping – discriminates against residents by non-residents.

No uniformity in common law – failed to create a center of gravity in federal common law.

There are differences in law, even within the same state.

Neither Congress nor federal courts have the power to declare the law for the states.

General lawmaking authority rests with the states unless there is an express grant of federal legislative authority.

Federal courts have no inherent lawmaking power unless authorized by Congress or courts.

The diversity clause does not empower Congress to make substantive law or delegate power to federal courts.

Guaranty Trust v. York (1945): York sued Guaranty Trust for self-interest. The statute of limitations barred the suit, but the federal court allowed suit; the Supreme Court reversed.

In equity, a federal court must use the statute of limitations of the state where it sits.

Outcome determinative test – if the result would change, use federal law; *Erie* uses state law.

A federal court in diversity is only another court of the state, but this was unworkable as a federal court would need to incorporate two sets of laws: one for federal and another for diversity.

Federal common law governs the claim preclusive effect of dismissal by a federal court sitting in diversity; no uniform federal rule.

The court must adopt a law that would be applied by state courts in the state in which the federal court sits.

Klaxon v. Senator Electrical (1941): NY substantive law (1st Restatement) was reversed by the Supreme Court.

Federal district court sitting in diversity must apply the law of the state where it sits and treat state choice-of-law questions like state substantive law questions.

Uniform administrability of the laws – there is no federal choice-of-law regime:

> prevents forum shopping- but federal courts in different states are not uniform, encouraging the plaintiff to bring suit in certain places,

> avoids renvoi (when a court is faced with a conflict of law and must consider the law of another state),

> disinterested forum – not overly bound by parochial rules.

Van Dusen v. Barrack (1964) – problems with *Klaxon*: defendant seeks to transfer to another court, and the transferee court must apply the state law that would have been applied if there is no change of venue.

The same rule applies if the plaintiff transfers the case (*Ferens v. John Deere*).

An act of Congress or the Supremacy Clause of the Constitution mandates enforcing U.S. law.

Testa v. Katt (1947): the Emergency Price Control Act – a buyer of goods may sue the seller in any court for not more than three times the overcharge and attorney's fees. The Rhode Island state court only awarded compensatory damages for the overcharge because the statute was penal and public policy exception not to enforce criminal statutes of foreign jurisdictions. The Supreme Court held that a state court must enforce a federal Act (supremacy) even if the state has a policy against enforcement.

A federal Act supersedes a countervailing policy of a state.

The U.S. does not bear the same relation to states as foreign jurisdictions.

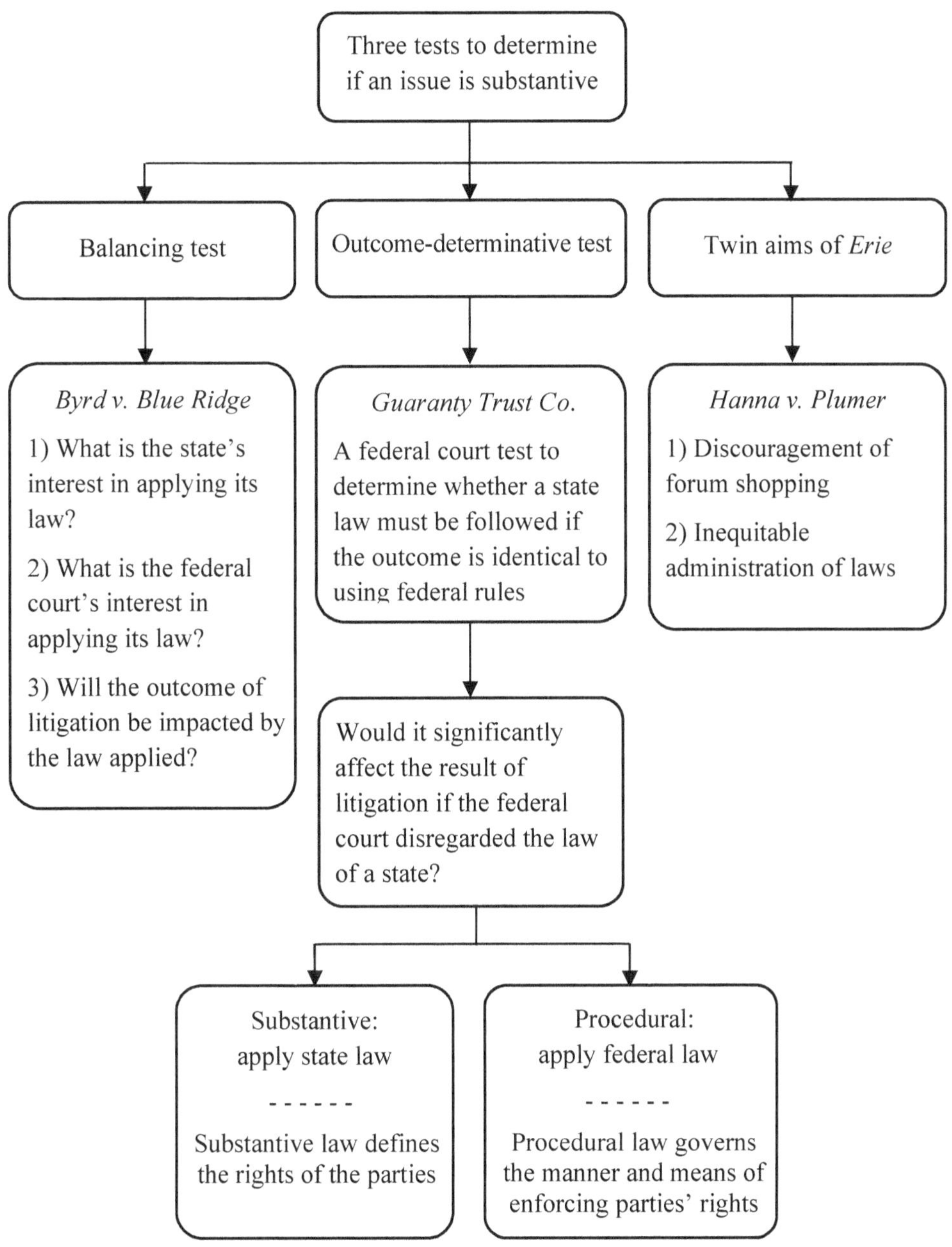

International conflicts

Full faith and credit does not apply between a foreign country and a U.S. state.

Limits of legislative jurisdiction in international law: jurisdiction to proscribe legislative jurisdiction recognizes states' authority to make substantive laws applicable to conduct relationships or status.

Territorial bases for jurisdiction over extraterritorial crimes under international law:

Territoriality – where the offense was committed,

Subjective – conduct occurs in the territory,

Objective – effects felt within a territory.

Protective jurisdiction is based on injury to the national interest. It has a narrow construction whereby the offenses are against the Secretary of State, the integrity of governmental functions (e.g., counterfeiting, espionage, passport fraud).

Universal jurisdiction is when the physical custody of the defendant that committed offenses impacts the entire world (e.g., privacy, state trade, hijacking, war crimes).

No jurisdiction if the exercise of authority is unreasonable.

Methods to define unreasonableness:

link of activity of the territory to the regulatory state,

connection.

The character of action to be regulated is important to the regulatory state:

justified expectation,

importance of regulations to the international political, economic, and legal system,

consistency of regulation with traditions of the international legal system,

when another state has intent in the regulatory Act,

likelihood of conflict with another state's regulation.

Comity (i.e., mutual recognition) reduces international friction.

Court must use legislative history, extra-statutory materials, canons of statutory construction.

Foley Brothers (1949) presumption – legislation of Congress, unless a contrary intent appears, is only meant to apply within the territorial jurisdiction of the U.S. and must be clearly stated:

congressional intent, and

reasonableness (comity) analysis.

Courts refrain from judging acts of a foreign government within their territory.

Territoriality – extraterritorial effects to a foreign state action.

Clear law – if clear local law prohibits the act, the doctrine does not apply. Not solely limited to government parties.

Abstention – a negative doctrine whereby courts do not adjudicate, but presume, the validity of foreign acts.

Full Faith and Credit for Foreign Judgments

Foreign judgments

Jurisdiction requirement: subject matter jurisdiction over the case and personal jurisdiction over the defendant or at least,

> full and fair opportunity to challenge jurisdiction,
>
> on the merits,
>
> final adjudication.

Requirements of the judgment:

> judgment must meet full faith and credit requirements, and
>
> no valid defenses apply.

Equitable decrees and obligation to enforce sister state judgments

The settlement is within the meaning of the full faith and credit clause because of the court's significant involvement in implementing the judgment.

Congress shall have the power to approve and effect full faith and credit (i.e., judgments from the courts of sister states).

U.S. Constitution Article IV § 1 – full faith and credit shall be given in each state to the public acts, records, and judicial proceedings of every other state.

28 U.S.C. § 1738 – requires federal courts give full faith and credit to state court judgments.

The Supreme Court has consistently required state courts to grant full faith and credit to federal court judgments.

The doctrine promotes judicial efficiency and justice.

Enforcing a claim in a foreign jurisdiction required a final judgment in the original state and an action to enforce it in another.

A final judgment (*res judicata*) in the original state is entitled to full faith and credit (*preclusion*) in the subsequent state:

> the original judgment must be valid (due process / personal jurisdiction),
>
> the original judgment must be final (e.g., adjustments of alimony are not final).

Some states permit modifications of foreign alimony judgments by statute (or judicial creation) for public policy to prevent a defendant from eluding a support obligation so the state will not have to care for the aggrieved party.

If a judgment is modifiable (e.g., future alimony or child support), it is not a final judgment but will usually be enforced under principles of comity.

Judgments for amounts already accrued and in arrears are considered final judgments.

The original judgment must have been decided on the merits (i.e., judgment involves the substance of the plaintiff's claim). Default and consent judgments are on the merits.

Dismissal for lack of jurisdiction (e.g., improper venue, *forum non conveniens*) is not on the merits.

Majority view: dismissals based upon laches and running of the statutes of limitations are not on the merits.

In federal court, a judgment can be registered in any district, making it enforceable and alleviating the need for a separate suit.

Most states have adopted similar provisions.

Full faith and credit must be given to wrongly decided cases since the proper remedy is appeal through the state's appellate process culminating with a *writ of certiorari* to the Supreme Court.

Full faith and credit to judicial proceedings of other nations

The recognizing state determines whether the foreign nation court had jurisdiction and used fair procedures.

Federal common law considerations favor enforcing a foreign nation's judgment (*Hilton v. Guyot*) when the:

> plaintiff and defendant are citizens of the foreign state,

> defendant is a citizen of the foreign state,

> plaintiff is a citizen of the foreign state, and judgment is for the defendant.

Reciprocity

Federal courts should recognize and enforce a foreign country's judgments if that country subjects an American judgment to similar treatment (*Hilton*).

Most states recognize foreign country judgments subject to the usual defenses and reject reciprocity (doctrine explicitly rejected by NY).

To avoid the majority rule, bring an action in a state that requires reciprocity and bring an enforcement action under full faith and credit.

Reciprocity is part of the federal common law and does not apply in diversity cases since the court was not deciding a federal question.

Reciprocity can be confined to a narrow holding – only when a foreign national prevails in a suit against a U.S. citizen.

Comity is the recognition one nation allows to the legislative, executive, or judicial acts of another government based upon mutual respect and cooperation among sovereign nations.

Limitations on full faith and credit

Full faith and credit does not apply to foreign nation judgments.

2nd Restatement of Conflicts § 103 Limitations on Full Faith and Credit: the court must have jurisdiction; otherwise, the judgment is not entitled to full faith and credit.

Full faith and credit does not oblige states to enforce (as opposed to recognizing) the judgments of sister states in the manner specified by that sister state's law.

Equitable judgment enforcement: full faith and credit does not mean the states must adopt the practices of other states regarding the time, manner, and mechanisms for enforcing judgments.

The enforcement measures do not travel with the sister state judgment as preclusive effects do; such measures remain subject to forum law control.

Exclusive jurisdiction over a federal cause of action granted by statute may partially repeal full faith and credit under 28 U.S.C. § 1738 (federal court recognition of a state court judgment).

A problem arises when a plaintiff brings a state cause of action in state court but cannot also assert their federal cause of action since Congress has granted the federal courts exclusive jurisdiction (e.g., antitrust, patent cases).

An award in one state should be entitled to full faith and credit, barring a second recovery in a sister state.

States need not respect a judgment affecting title to land located in their state when another state renders judgment.

A divorce decree issued in the original state that vests title to property located in a different state does not have to be recognized in that state for a quiet title action.

If a spouse brought an action to enforce the original judgment in another state, the outcome would likely be different since there is no reason not to enforce an equity decree.

Baker v. General Motors (US 1998) – exceptions to full faith and credit:

>an original judgment that purports to accomplish an official act within the exclusive province of another state (e.g., deeding of land),

>injunctions interfering with litigation over which the ordering state has no authority,

>if the plaintiff is held in contempt of the subsequent court (highly criticized opinion).

Limitations imposed by the state of the transaction

States determine the competency of their courts and are not bound by limitations on jurisdiction imposed by the law of a sister state.

State statutes that localize a transitory cause of action and grant exclusive jurisdiction to its local courts do not prohibit a sister state court from asserting jurisdiction.

The judgment from the sister state is entitled to full faith and credit, unless:

>anti-suit injunctions are based upon such a statute,

>a forum is not compelled to accept the jurisdiction of a cause of action created under a sister state's laws.

State administrative agency determinations that have not been judicially reviewed are not given issue preclusion effect.

Recognition of Foreign Judgments

Claim preclusion

Res judicata (claim preclusion) prohibits a second suit on a claim or cause of action, which was asserted in prior litigation and resulted in a valid, final judgment on the merits.

Claim preclusion prevents a party from relitigating an entire suit when:

1) final judgment on the first suit is entered,

2) the same cause of action as the first suit,

3) same subject matter and ultimate issue,

4) the second suit seeks relief for the same harm,

5) same parties or their privies,

6) successors in interest or holders of future interests, or

7) beneficiaries of actual parties.

Persons bound by *res judicata* are parties to the action and those in privity with them.

Privity by a person so closely related to a party that it is fair to bind them to the litigation (e.g., trustee and beneficiary of a trust, successive property owners regarding an easement).

Issue preclusion

Collateral estoppel (issue preclusion) prohibits relitigating issues decided in a prior proceeding regardless of whether the second proceeding is based upon the same cause of action.

In a second suit on a different cause of action, issues litigated and decided are precluded from relitigating if:

1) the issue was litigated in the first proceeding,

2) the issue was necessary to support the judgment of the first proceeding,

3) the party against whom collateral estoppel is asserted was a prior party or privy in the first proceeding,

4) the party had a full and fair opportunity to litigate the issue in the prior proceeding.

Federal law controls the preclusive effects of federal court judgments regardless of whether the court was exercising federal question or diversity jurisdiction (majority view).

If a defendant makes a limited appearance for an *in rem* or *quasi in rem* proceeding (e.g., foreclosed mortgage) in court and the parties litigate the merits, that court's findings on issues litigated preclude subsequent relitigating of those issues in a different court even though the first court lacked personal jurisdiction over the defendant.

If a defendant appears specially, and the court determines that it has personal jurisdiction, the defendant cannot claim a lack of jurisdiction to prevent full faith and credit in another court.

Similarly, subject matter jurisdiction issues are precluded if fully and fairly litigated.

Mutuality of estoppel

Claim and issue preclusion will not be applied to the detriment of strangers to the litigation since they were not provided notice and given the opportunity to be heard.

If a court with property-based jurisdiction exceeds its limited powers and purports to issue a personal judgment against a defendant, that judgment is not entitled to full faith and credit.

Unless it has personal jurisdiction over a debtor, the court cannot issue a deficiency judgment

A court with *in rem* jurisdiction is limited to issuing preclusive judgments regarding the *res* (i.e., item of real or personal property) only.

Class suits: a judgment is binding on members of the class whenever they may later bring suit on the same cause of action, if:

1) absent members of the class were adequately represented in the litigation, and

2) a reasonable number of the class were given adequate notice of the suit and had an opportunity to be heard.

Defenses to Recognition or Enforcement

Defenses against application of foreign law

Comity of nations – a court gives deference (not an obligation) to a foreign decision.

Requirements to recognize judgment – preconditions to acceptance of comity:

1) full and fair trial,

2) court of competent jurisdiction,

3) a trial conducted through regular proceedings,

4) adequate notice to defendant (English),

5) impartial justice between citizens and aliens.

There is no prejudice in a court of laws against foreign judgments; the difference between the foreign and U.S. systems is due process violation but will not block enforcement. This is a less demanding standard than an international measure of due process.

There must be no fraud in procuring the judgment and no reason for denying comity.

§ 4 Uniform Foreign Money Judgment Recognition Acts

Section 4 foreign judgments are entitled to full faith and credit if requirements are met.

The judgment must not be rendered under a system that did not provide impartial tribunals or procedures compatible with due process requirements.

Mandatory defenses – judgment will not be enforced when:

1) no personal jurisdiction over the defendant,

2) no subject matter jurisdiction.

Discretionary defenses – judgment may not be enforced when:

1) no notice within sufficient time,

2) judgment obtained by fraud,

3) violation of public policy,

4) the judgment conflicts with another final and conclusive judgment,

5) violation of an agreement between the parties,

6) inconvenient forum.

Notes for active learning

Nature of Original Proceedings

Foreign country judgments

Jurisdiction must have been proper, and fair procedures must have been used in the foreign country proceeding.

Apply the recognizing state's law – the state's idea of due process (e.g., minimum contacts, fair play, and substantial justice).

Defenses against a foreign nation judgment emanate from public policy, which is broader application than in domestic matters and international law that an American court cannot recognize (e.g., slavery).

State law determines the effect of foreign nation judgments on American courts.

Lack of personal or subject matter jurisdiction makes a judgment void and not entitled to full faith and credit. Challenges to jurisdictional determinations are made in the rendering state's appellate process and eventually by *writ* to the Supreme Court.

By bringing an action in a court, the plaintiff is submitting to the court's jurisdiction. Therefore, the judgment will have a preclusive effect against the plaintiff in an action in another court.

A mere recital of jurisdiction is conclusory and insufficient. The recital of jurisdictional facts upon which jurisdiction was based is not enough to preclude the issue.

Inconsistent judgments – full faith and credit must be accorded to a court judgment even if that judgment fails to give full faith and credit to a prior court judgment. This creates a last-in-time rule for the applicability of judgments.

When the third forum is also the first, the Supreme Court requires recognition of the second forum's judgment.

Lack of finality (common in domestic relations cases) – not entitled to full faith and credit.

Final judgments such as for payment of past alimony must be given effect in another court.

Accrued alimony is not yet reduced to a judgment if:

> the original court modifies alimony awards prospectively; accrued alimony is not modifiable and subject to enforcement in the subsequent court,

> the original court retrospectively modifies alimony.

Modifiable judgments are not final, but subsequent courts exercise discretion enforcing them.

The plaintiff is not disadvantaged if they are accorded due process.

Modifiable judgments eliminate the undue burden on the plaintiff of having to return to the original court to obtain a final judgment.

Extrinsic fraud could not have been addressed within the earlier trial (e.g., bribing a judge).

With extrinsic fraud, the defendant was deprived of the opportunity to litigate, and the subsequent court does not have to grant full faith and credit to a judgment obtained by fraud.

Intrinsic fraud (e.g., perjury of a witness) could have been addressed during litigation and is not a good defense to full faith and credit.

With intrinsic fraud, a collateral attack is not available regarding fraud that the resisting party had an opportunity to litigate in the original court.

If the original court's law allows a collateral attack, the subsequent court may address the issue by applying its procedural rules.

Full faith and credit may be denied for a judgment based on a cause of action that violates the forum's public policy.

For mistakes by the judge in the earlier trial, the proper remedy is an appeal.

Later judgment can be enforced even though it is inconsistent with a valid earlier one. The rule is to enforce the last judgment.

Defenses – nature of the original cause of action

Penal judgments are not entitled to full faith and credit and are narrowly defined:

> the purpose is to punish rather than compensate, and

> recovery is in favor of the state.

Penal damages do not include:

> punitive damages if recovery favors an individual,

> wrongful death awards even where the defendant's fault is the measure of recovery.

Judgments not entitled to full faith and credit:

> a tort judgment in favor of a state's proprietary interests,

> a tax judgment since the purpose is the generation of revenue.

Judgments based upon mistake of fact or law are nonetheless entitled to full faith and credit.

The subsequent court must recognize the other court's judgment even if the original court erroneously interpreted the subsequent court's law, and it has an interest in the activity (*Fauntleroy v. Lum* 1908 – judgment enforced a "futures" trading agreement illegal in the forum).

The forum can apply its statute of limitations barring action from enforcing a judgment even though shorter than the original court's statute of limitations. This is an exception to the rule applying at least as much credit to a judgment as the original forum.

The statute of limitations on enforcing foreign judgments can be shorter than the statute of limitations for domestic judgments if an action in the foreign state can revive the foreign judgment. The time limit begins on the date of the last foreign transaction.

A state cannot refuse to enforce a sister state judgment on the ground that the original action could not have been brought in the state in which enforcement is sought (e.g., lacked subject matter jurisdiction over the original cause of action).

The subsequent court is merely enforcing a judgment, and it is irrelevant that the claim could not have been brought there.

Notes for active learning

Family Law Judgments

Types of divorce

Ex parte divorce – only one of the spouses is validly domiciled, where the divorce is granted. The decree does not govern collateral matters (e.g., property, alimony, support, custody).

Bi-lateral divorce – one of the spouses is validly domiciled, where the divorce is granted, and each is subject to personal jurisdiction there.

Consent divorce – parties want out of the marriage and go somewhere to get divorced ("quickie divorce"). This divorce is not valid if neither spouse is domiciled in the jurisdiction that granted it.

Family law judgments

Termination of marital status (divorce decree) must have proper subject matter jurisdiction.

One spouse must be domiciled in the state rendering the divorce.

Divorce judgments: decree is valid as to the divorce.

The general rule is to give full faith and credit if:

> proper jurisdiction,

> a decree is valid in the sister state,

> decree valid as to the divorce.

Jurisdiction is proper if at least one party is domiciled in the rendering state.

Procedural matters on divorce

The plaintiff bears the burden of proof.

Parties may introduce relevant evidence even if the evidence came into existence after the divorce was granted.

Any interested person who is not estopped can attack the divorce decree for lack of subject matter jurisdiction.

Estoppel for divorce

Estoppel applies to the challenger subject to personal jurisdiction in the earlier proceeding (spouse in a bi-lateral divorce cannot challenge divorce).

> The challenger played a meaningful role in the granting of the divorce, even without personal jurisdiction.

> The spouse remarried in reliance on the earlier divorce.

> Persons in privity with a party to the divorce include children.

Property awards (e.g., alimony, child support) must have personal jurisdiction over a spouse whose property rights are in issue.

Valid jurisdiction for determining child custody lies only in the child's home state.

Divisible divorce doctrine

Divisible divorce – the marriage is dissolved, but the incident issues (e.g., alimony, child custody, visitation) are reserved until a later proceeding.

This type of divorce is granted when the court has subject matter jurisdiction but lacks personal jurisdiction over the defendant (only one party domiciled in the state).

If the decree has some valid parts and others not, the valid parts hold, and remainder disregarded.

Relationship matrix

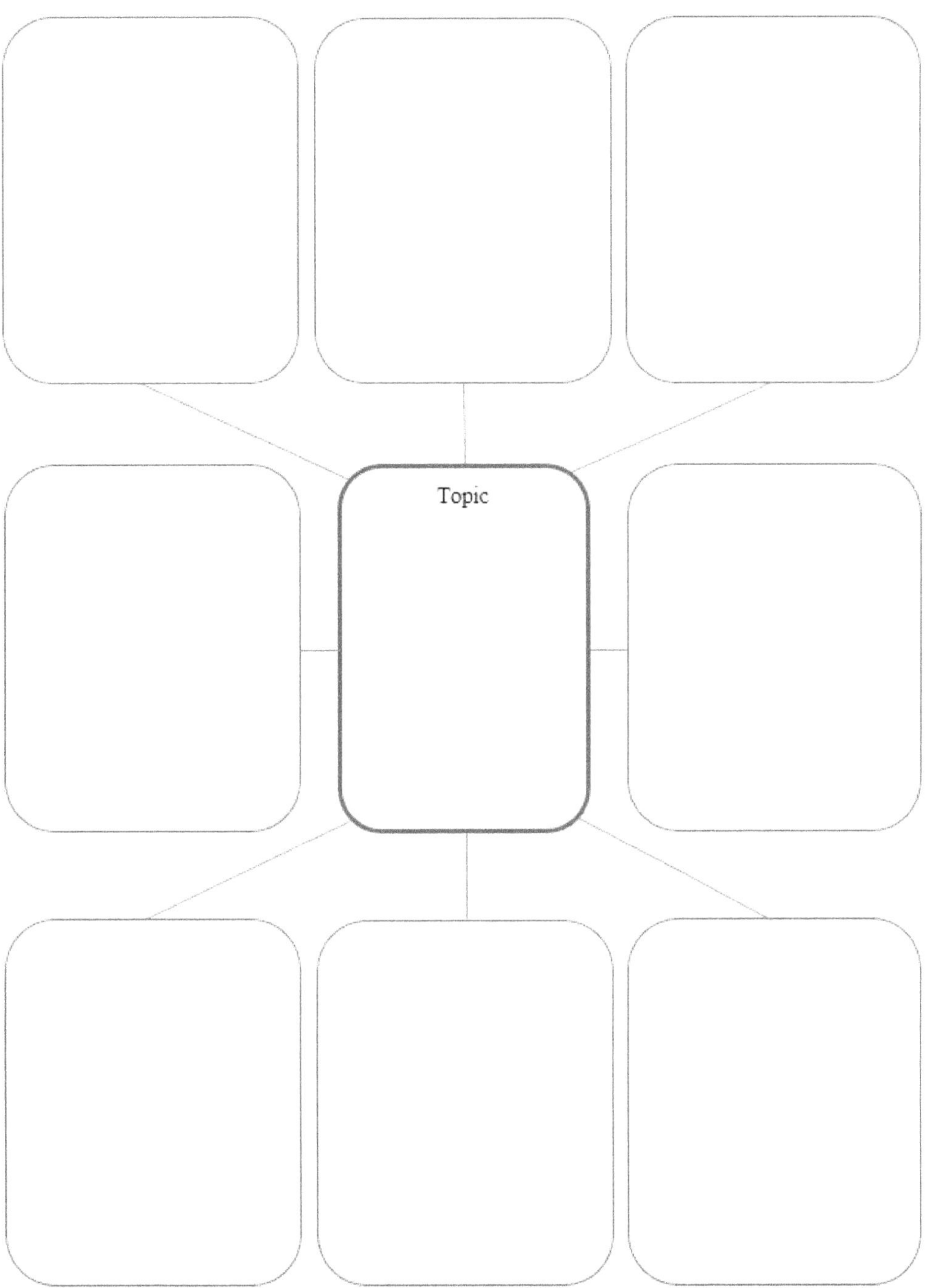

Notes for active learning

Notes for active learning

Notes for active learning

Bar Exam Information, Preparation
and
Test-Taking Strategies

STERLING
Test Prep

Introduction to the Uniform Bar Examination (UBE)

Structure of the UBE

The Uniform Bar Examination (UBE) includes 1) the Multistate Bar Examination (MBE), 2) Multistate Essay Examination (MEE), and 3) Multistate Performance Test (MPT).

The MBE has 200 multiple-choice questions accounting for 50% of the UBE.

The MEE has six essays worth 30% of the UBE score.

The MPT has two legal tasks (e.g., complaint, client letter) for 20% of the UBE score.

The Multistate Bar Examination (MBE)

The Multistate Bar Examination consists of 200 four-option multiple-choice questions prepared by the National Conference of Bar Examiners (NCBE).

Of these 200 questions, 175 are scored, and 25 are unscored pretest questions.

Candidates answer 100 questions in the three-hour morning session and the remaining 100 questions in the three-hour afternoon session.

The 175 scored questions are distributed with 25 questions on each of the seven subject areas: Federal Civil Procedure, Constitutional Law, Contracts, Criminal Law and Procedure, Evidence, Real Property, and Torts.

A specified percentage of questions in each subject tests topics in those subjects.

For example, approximately one-third of Evidence questions test hearsay and its exceptions, while approximately one-third of Torts questions test negligence.

Interpreting the UBE score report

Overall score. The National Conference of Bar Examiners (NCBE) states the Uniform Bar Exam (UBE) requires a passing scaled score between 260 to 280. Scores above 280 receive a passing score in every UBE state.

The "percentile" is the number of people that scored lower. If an examinee scored in the 47th percentile, they scored higher than 47% of the examinees (and lower than 53%).

The examinee is first given a "raw score,"; based on the number of correct answers.

The raw score is adjusted by adding points to achieve the "scaled score." The number of points added is determined by a formula that compares the difficulty of the current exam to prior benchmark exams.

The comparative performance of examinees on "control questions" (prior pretest questions) given on previous exams form the basis for determining each exam's difficulty.

MBE scaled score. Examinees receive a scaled score and not an MBE "raw" score (i.e., the number of correct answers). MBE scores are scaled scores calculated by the NCBE through a statistical process used for standardized tests.

According to the NCBE, this statistical process adjusts raw scores on the current exam to account for differences in difficulty compared to previously administered exams. The scaled score is calculated from the raw score, but the NCBE does not publish the conversion formula.

Since the MBE is a scaled score, equating makes it impossible to know precisely how many questions must be answered correctly to receive a particular score. Equating allows scores from different exams to be compared since a specific scaled score represents the same level of knowledge among exams.

The MBE is curved, so just because a score is "close" to passing does not mean you are close. For example, a 124 may be in the 31st percentile and a 136 in the 62nd percentile. A 12-point difference in scaled scores equates to a 31-point percentile difference. If you are in the 120s, much preparation is needed to increase your score.

For most states, aim for a scaled score of 135 to "pass" the MBE. If you are unsure what score you need, divide the passing score by two. For example, if a 270 is needed to pass the bar, divide 268 by two to yield 135 as a threshold score on the MBE.

The importance of the MBE score

A passing MBE score depends on the jurisdiction. In jurisdictions that score on a 200-point scale, the passing score is the overall score. Passing scores are often approximately 135.

For the July 2020 bar exam, the national average MBE score was 146.1, an increase of 5 points from the July 2019 national average of 141.1.

For comparison, on the July 2018 bar, the national average MBE score was 139.5, a decrease of about 2.2 points from the July 2017 national average of 141.7.

How much the MBE contributes depends on the jurisdiction. Each jurisdiction has its policy for the relative weight given to the MBE compared to other bar exam components.

For Uniform Bar Examination (UBE) jurisdictions, the MBE component is 50%.

Most jurisdictions combine the MBE score with the state essay exam score.

The overall state candidates' performance on the MBE controls the raw state essay's conversion to scaled scores. Achieve a scaled MBE score of at least 135 to pass the bar.

MEE and MPT scores

In a UBE score report, there are six scores for the Multistate Essay Exam (MEE) and two for the Multistate Performance Test (MPT). Most states release this information.

Most states grade on a 1–6 scale (some use another scale).

In states grading on a 1–6 scale, 4 is considered a passing score.

The MEE and MPT sections are not weighted equally.

The MEE essays are worth 60%, while the MPT is 40% of the written score.

Many examinees assume that they passed the MPT and MEE portions of the exam. Examine the score report to see how you performed on these portions.

The objective of the Multistate Bar Exam

Working knowledge of the MBE objectives, the skills it tests, how it is drafted, the relationship of the parts of an MBE question, and the testing limitations provide you a substantial advantage in choosing the correct answers to MBE questions and passing the bar.

Knowing which issues are tested and the form in which they are tested makes it more manageable to learn the large body of substantive law.

The MBE's fundamental objective is to measure fairly, and efficiently which law school graduates have the necessary academic qualifications to be admitted to the bar and exceed this threshold.

The multiple-choice exam used to accomplish this objective must be of a consistent level of difficulty.

The level at which the pass decision is made must be achievable by most candidates.

The MBE tests the following skills:

- reading carefully and critically
- identifying the legal issue in a set of facts
- knowing the law that governs the legal issues tested
- distinguish between frequently confused closely-related principles
- making reasonable judgments from ambiguous facts
- understanding how limiting words make plausible-sounding choices wrong
- choosing the correct answer by intelligently eliminating incorrect choices

Notes for active learning

Preparation Strategies for the Bar Exam

An effective bar exam study plan

There are a lot of great ideas about how to prepare. Follow through with these ideas and turn them into persistent action for successful preparation.

A detailed and well-planned study schedule has benefits, such as giving you a sense of control and building confidence and proficiency.

Pick a date about 12-14 weeks before the exam (November for the February exam and April for the July exam) and use it as the start of your active study period.

Start a month earlier than many others to have a month to review as final preparation at the end.

Students have found this effective. Use an elongated prep period as a study schedule.

Most examinees prefer at least two weeks before the exam to review the material.

By planning early, you will have more time. You may want three or four final weeks to review subjects, take timed exams, and ensure that you are prepared to take the exam.

A few notes on schedule management:

> Do not *start* memorizing during your initial review period. You should be learning every week from the beginning of your study schedule. This final prep period is for reviewing and taking timed exams.

> If you stretch the study schedule over several months, plan review weeks into your schedule. For example, every four weeks, use a few days to review the governing law and take timed exams. This is a practical and fruitful approach as you will be more likely to retain the information.

Pick specific dates for specific tasks; this makes it more likely you will complete them.

Make sure the tasks are measurable. (e.g., practice two MEE essays).

Be realistic about the tasks, time, energy, and your ability to complete the items listed as tasks in preparation for the exam.

Remember to take some scheduled breaks from studying.

Exercise, sleep and take care of your physical and mental health.

If you are not in the right mental state preparing for the exam, you will likely be ineffective when studying and are less likely to pass the exam.

Focused studying

Some people are better at multiple-choice questions; others do better with essays.

The multiple-choice portion (MBE at 50%) and the essay portion (MEE at 30% and MPT at 20%) are weighted equally.

Doing poorly in one section means it will be challenging to achieve a passing score.

Identify weaknesses early in the preparation process and focus on them.

If you struggle with multiple-choice questions, dedicate extra time to practicing MBE questions.

If you struggle with writing, focus on completing MEE essays and complete MPT practice materials.

By reviewing your performance on released multiple-choice practice tests, be concerned if you consistently miss questions that are most answered correctly.

If you have problems with questions and perform below 50%, you lack the fundamental knowledge necessary to pass the MBE.

When reviewing your answers to practice questions, it is essential to review all questions and answers, even those you got right.

Make sure you got that correct answer for the right reason.

Reviewing the questions and answers is critical for success on the exam.

Spend time reviewing those basic principles and working deliberately on the straightforward (and easy) questions that supplement learning.

Advice on using outlines

As a user of this governing law book, several of the following points are moot. They are included, so you can be confident that you are using the proper resources to prep for the bar.

Having a useful governing law study guide (such as this book) is critical.

Without effective resources, it is challenging to understand, learn and apply the governing law to the facts given in the question.

Some students use outlines that make learning difficult.

A few common mistakes about outlines:

- Learning outlines that are too long (e.g., more than 100 pages per subject) or too short (e.g., a seven-page Contracts outline). You will be overwhelmed by information or never learn enough governing law.

- Spending too much time comparing several outlines for the same subject.

  For example, using different Contracts outlines and needlessly comparing them. This confusion results in an undue focus on insignificant discrepancies.

- Outlining every subject. If you are not starting to study early, this consumes too much study time. Do not attempt to outline all subjects. It may be a good idea to outline a select few problematic subjects.

Using a detailed and well-organized governing law outline (e.g., this book) is essential; it saves time, organizes concepts, reduces anxiety, and helps you score well and pass the bar.

Easy questions make the difference

Limitations on the examiners lead to the first important insight into preparation for the exam – the kind of questions that decide whether you pass.

Performance on specific questions correlates with success or failure on the bar.

By analyzing statistics, questions predicting success or failure have been identified.

In general, the most challenging questions were not particularly good predictors of failure because most people who missed them passed the bar.

However, many of the straightforward questions were excellent predictors of success.

The median raw score ranges from about 60% to 66% correct on the MBE.

The National Conference of Bar Examiners (NCBE) writes, "expert panelists reported that they believed MBE items were generally easy, correctly estimating that about 66% of candidates would select the right answer to a typical item."

Depending on the exam's difficulty, in most states, scoring slightly below the median (miss up to 80 questions) still passes.

The most important questions to determine if you pass are not the exceedingly challenging ones but the easy ones where 90% of the examinees answer correctly.

The easy questions usually test a basic and regularly tested point of substantive law.

The wrong choices (i.e., the distracters) are typically easy to eliminate.

Your first task in preparing for the MBE is to get easy questions correct.

Study plan based upon statistics

These statistics show that an excellent performance on either the MBE questions (approximately 67% correct) or the state essays (4s on essays) assures you a passing score.

If you fail the MBE by 9 points or the essays by 5 points, the probability of passing the bar is in the single digits.

Put effort into performing well on the MBE questions for the following reasons.

- The questions are objective, and there are enough questions that are predictable concerning content and structure that it is possible, through reasonable effort, to answer 67% of the questions correctly.

- Studying the MBE first has the added advantage of preparing the necessary substantive law for state essays.

- The essays cover several subjects, the precise topic tested is unpredictable, and the answers are graded subjectively by graders who work quickly.

You had three years of law school practice with essays and less experience with multiple-choice questions.

Master the MBE before spending time preparing for the essays.

Factors associated with passing the bar

Based on an analysis of statistics from students' performance, the following factors predict the likelihood of passing the bar:

LSAT score

First-year Grade Point Average (GPA)

LSAT scores are a significant predictor of success on the bar because the LSAT requires similar multiple-choice test-taking skills as the MBE.

The LSAT tests many of the types of legal reasoning tested on the MBE.

A lower LSAT can be overcome by a comprehensive study of the MBE governing law, but these students must work harder.

Most of the subjects tested (e.g., constitutional law, civil procedure, contracts, criminal law, real property, torts) on the MBE are taken in the first year of law school.

First-year GPA measures mastery of subjects, preparedness for exams, and the ability to understand legal principles and apply them to given fact patterns.

The MBE measures the same factors but in a multiple-choice format instead of essays.

Pass rates based on GPA and LSAT scores

Past statistics indicate that law students with LSAT scores above 155 and a first-year GPA above 3.0 are reasonably assured of passing the bar.

They should study conscientiously and take practice MBEs to perform at the level needed, but they have little cause to panic.

Students with LSAT scores between 150 and 155 and a first-year GPA between 2.5 and 3.0 are in a bit more danger of failing and need to undertake rigorous preparation.

They must achieve a scaled score of 135 and take released practice exams and understand the reasons for incorrect choices. They should prepare for state essays by learning the governing laws in this book.

Students with LSAT scores between 145 and 150 and a first-year GPA between 2.2 and 2.5 have a moderate chance of passing the bar from deliberate efforts.

These students should not rely on ordinary commercial bar reviews and need intense training, particularly on the MBE component of the bar. They must devote 50-60 hours per week for seven weeks to prepare for the bar by learning the format and content of substantive law tested on the MBE. They should take released practice exams under exam conditions and conscientiously study the questions missed.

Students with LSAT scores below 145 and a GPA below 2.2 have had a failure rate of approximately 80%.

They must prep faithfully and conscientiously beyond the advice above and must engage in a rigorous course of study, more than is demanded by a traditional bar review course.

Notes for active learning

Learning and Applying the Substantive Law

Knowledge of substantive law

The fundamental reason for missing a question is 1) a failure to know the principle of law controlling the answer or 2) failure to understand how that principle is applied.

You must know and apply the governing law to pass the bar. If you do not know the governing law, you will not apply it to answer correctly.

Many students *think* they understand the governing law but do not know the nuances. Do not assume that you understand the governing (i.e., substantive) law. It is prevalent for students not to know the governing law well.

Re-learn the substantive and procedural law taught in first-year courses.

A major mistake is not to memorize the governing law outlined in this book.

The multiple-choice and essay portions test nuances and details of governing law. It is essential to analyze the governing law as it is applied in the context of the question.

On the multiple-choice section, many questions require fine-line distinctions between similar principles of law.

Several multiple-choice answers will *seem* correct, given the limited time to answer. If your knowledge of the governing law is suboptimal, you will not make these subtle distinctions and will have to guess on many questions.

For the essay to be developed, you must know the governing law and apply it to the issues within the call of the question.

If you do not know the governing law, you will not state the correct rule in your essay. You will be unable to apply the correct rule to the fact pattern.

Where to find the law

The questions must be related to the subject matter outlined in the bar examiners' (NCBE) materials.

While the NCBE outline is broad and ambiguous, years of experience with the exam delineate the scope of material you must learn.

The governing law covered in this book is foundational to the exam. The governing law statements were compiled by analyzing questions released by the multistate examiners. The analysis revealed a limited number of legal principles repeatedly tested.

Review these principles before taking practice exams and understand how they are applied to obtain the correct answer.

The property questions are probably the most difficult. The fact patterns are usually long and involve many parties in complex transactions.

In preparing for the exam, learn basic property principles and apply them. However, extensive studying into property law's crevices is not necessary to score well on these questions.

Feel confident that you do not have to go beyond the information provided in this book to find the governing law.

Controlling authority

The examiners have specified the sources of authority for the correct answers.

In Constitutional Law and Criminal Procedure, it is Supreme Court decisions.

In Criminal Law, it is common law.

In Evidence, the Federal Rules of Evidence controls.

In Torts and Property, it is the generally accepted view of United States law.

The UCC is the controlling authority in sales (Article 2) questions.

The NCBE released questions, and the published answers determine the controlling law through deduction.

Recent changes in the law

The exam is prepared months before it is given because of logistical requirements. Therefore, the examiners cannot incorporate recent changes in the law into the questions.

Recent changes in the law will not form the basis for correct answers.

If a recent change makes an answer initially designated as the correct answer to be incorrect, the examiners will credit more than one answer.

The recent holding of a Supreme Court case will not be tested for about two years since the decision was published.

Lesser-known issues and unusual applications

Some of the challenging exam questions are based on obscure principles of law.

Missing the most challenging questions will not cause you to fail the exam if you have a solid understanding of the governing law. You can learn these principles and answer the question correctly, thereby improving your overall performance.

There are instances where the correct answers are different from the usual rules.

For example, hearsay evidence inadmissible at trial is admissible before a judge hearing evidence on a preliminary question of fact (e.g., Federal Rules of Evidence 104(a)).

Practice applying the governing law

Some students know the governing law but have problems *applying* it to the facts.

The exam is as much about testing skills as it is about testing the governing law.

Therefore, knowledge of the governing law is not enough to pass.

You must practice answering multiple-choice questions and writing well-organized, coherent, and complete essays where you apply the governing law to the given facts.

Know which governing law is being tested

A typical wrong answer (i.e., distracter) on a question is an answer which is correct under a body of law other than the governing law being tested.

An example is a question governed by Article 2 of the Uniform Commercial Code (UCC), where an offer is irrevocable if:

1) it is in writing,

2) made by a merchant, and

3) states that it is irrevocable.

One of the wrong answers states the correct rule under the common law of contracts, where an offer is revocable unless consideration is paid (i.e., an option) for the promise to keep it open.

Answers which are always wrong

Some commonly used distracters are always wrong and can be eliminated quickly.

For example, a choice in an evidence question says, "character can only be attacked by reputation evidence." This choice is wrong because both opinion and reputation evidence is admissible under the Federal Rules of Evidence when character attacks are permissible.

Honing Reading Skills

Reading skills are critical. The basic level is reading to understand the facts, identify the issue and keep the parties distinct. A mistake at this juncture results in answering incorrectly, no matter how much law is known.

Understanding complex transactions

If the question involves a transaction with many parties, diagram the transaction before analyzing the choices.

The diagram should show the relationship between the parties (e.g., grantor-grantee, assignor-assignee), the transaction date, and the person's relationships in the transaction (e.g., donee, *bona fide* purchaser).

Impediments to careful reading

Two reasons candidates fail to read carefully are:

1) hurrying through a question,

2) fatigue due to a lack of sleep or strain caused by the exam.

A careful test taker maintains a steady, deliberate pace during the exam. Practice in advance and be well-rested on the test day.

Reading too much into a question

The examiners are committed to designing questions, which are "a fair index of whether the applicant has the ability to practice law." Psychometric experts ensure that they are fair and unbiased.

Even though you must read every word of these carefully drafted questions, do not read the question to find some bizarre interpretation.

The examiners must ask fair questions and not rely on "tricks." Reading too much into a question and looking for a trick lurking behind every fact leads to the wrong answer often.

It is the straightforward questions that determine whether you pass, not the occasional challenging question that tests some arcane principle of law.

Therefore, take questions at face value.

Read the call of the question first

Before reading the facts, read the call of the question because it indicates the task for selecting the correct answer. This perspective focuses your attention before reading the facts.

The question contains many *words of art*, such as "most likely," "best defense," or "least likely," which govern the correct answer.

The call is often phrased positively; the "best argument" or "most likely result."

Read answers for consistency with the question and eliminate inconsistent choices.

Negative calls

When the call of the question is negative, asking for the "weakest argument" or asking which of the options is "not" in a specified category, examine each option with the perspective that the choice with those negative characteristics is the correct answer.

After reading and understanding the question stem, read the call of the question again before reading the choices.

Analyze each choice with the requirements specified in the call of the question.

Read all choices

Never pick an answer until carefully reading all the choices. The objective is to pick the best answer, which cannot be determined until comparing the choices.

Sometimes the difference between the right and wrong answer is that one choice is more detailed or precisely sets forth the applicable law. You do not know that until reading all the answers carefully.

Broad statements of black letter law may be correct

When reading an answer, do not rule out choices with imprecise statements of the applicable *black letter* law.

If the examiners always included a choice that was precisely on point, the questions would be too easy. Instead, they often disguise the wording used in the correct answer.

For example, the Federal Rules of Evidence contain an elaborate set of relevancy rules that limit the right to introduce evidence of repairs after an accident. If there was a question where the introduction of that evidence was permissible, and no choices specifically cite the exception to the general rule of exclusion, an answer phrased with the general rule of relevancy "Admissible because its probative value outweighs its prejudicial effect," would be the correct answer.

Multiple-Choice Test-Taking Tactics

Determine the single correct answer

Increase the odds of picking the correct answer based on technical factors independent of substantive (governing) law knowledge.

The examiners' limitation is that every question must have one demonstrably correct and three demonstrably incorrect answers, limiting how the examiners write the choices.

From the question's construction, this limitation may give clues about the answer.

Process of elimination

Answering a multiple-choice question is not finding the ideal answer to the question asked but instead picking the best option.

Eliminate choices and evaluate the remaining choice for plausibility.

Eliminate choices that state an incorrect proposition of law or do not relate to the facts.

If you eliminate three options and the remaining one is acceptable, pick it and move on.

Elimination increases the odds

It takes about 125 correct answers to pass the MBE. An important strategy in reaching that number is intelligently eliminating choices.

If you are sure of the answer to only 50 of the 200 questions on the exam and confidently eliminate two of the four choices on the remaining 150 questions. Guess between the two remaining choices, and the odds predict 75 correct.

Those 75 correct, coupled with 50 questions you were confident of the answer, produce a raw score of 125 on the MBE and a scaled score above the benchmark 135.

Unfortunately, you cannot avoid guessing on questions, but intelligent methods reduce options to only two viable choices.

Sometimes you might not be able to eliminate the wrong answers just because you are sure of the answer to one of the choices. Eliminating with confidence even one choice increases the probability of correctly answering the question.

Eliminating two wrong answers

Specific questions on the MBE are challenging because of distinguishing between two choices when selecting the best answer.

A typical comment from examinees leaving the exam is, "I could not decide between the last two choices."

The positive side of that problem is eliminating two of the four choices.

Pick the winning side

The most common choice pattern is the "two-two" pattern – two choices state that the plaintiff prevails, and two that the defendant prevails.

The best approach for this type of question is to rely on your knowledge of the law or instinctive feeling to which conclusion is correct.

In a question with two choices on one side and two on the other side of a court's decision, first, pick a choice on the side you think should prevail.

Distinguish between the explanations following this conclusion and pick the choice that best justifies it.

Distance between choices on the other side

If the justifications following the conclusion for the side you chose seem indistinguishable, look at the explanations for the choices on the other side.

If the reasons for the choices on the other side are readily distinguishable, and one appears reasonable and the other incorrect, reconsider your initial conclusion.

Remember, the examiner is required to provide a distinguishable reason why one explanation of a general conclusion is correct, and the other is wrong.

That obligation does not exist if the general conclusion itself is incorrect.

Suppose choices (A) and (B) on one side look correct; that is, they are reasonable and consistent with the fact pattern. One of the choices with the opposite conclusion, answer (C), seems incorrect or inconsistent with the facts, and answer (D) with the same general conclusion sounds reasonable. From a strictly technical viewpoint, the best choice is answer (D).

Questions based upon a common fact pattern

There are several instances where two or more questions are based on the same facts.

Look at the second question's wording to guide the first question's correct answer. When asked to assume an answer to a first question from a fact pattern to answer the second question, the probability is high that the answer to the first question follows that assumption.

For example, if the first question has two choices beginning with "P prevails" and two with "D prevails," and the second question starts with "If P prevails," it is likely one of the "P prevails" choices is correct for the first question. If you picked "D prevails," think carefully before selecting it as the final answer.

Multiple true/false issues

In addition to true/false questions, the exam sometimes states three propositions in the root of the question and tests characteristics of those propositions in the call of the question.

The choices list various combinations of propositions.

The difference between this type of question and the double true/false question is that only four of the eight possible combinations fit into the options. It is possible to answer correctly even if you are not sure of all propositions' truth or falsity but are sure of one.

Correctly stated, but the inapplicable principle of law

The task of the examiners is to make the wrong choices look attractive. A creative way to accomplish this is to write a choice that impeccably states a rule of law that is not applicable because of facts in the root of the question.

For example, in a question where a person is an assignee, not a sublessee, one of the choices may correctly state the law for sublessees, but it is inapplicable to the fact pattern.

Therefore, these answer choices with inapplicable law can be confidently eliminated.

"Because" questions

Conjunctions are commonly used in the answers. It is essential to understand their role in determining whether a choice is correct.

The word "because" connects a conclusion and the reason for that conclusion with the facts in the body of the question.

There are two requirements for a question using "because" to be correct:

1) the conclusion must be correct,

2) the reasoning must logically follow based upon facts in the question, and the statement which follows "because" must be legally correct.

If the "because" choice has the correct result for the wrong reason, it is incorrect.

"If" questions

The conjunction "if" requires a much narrower focus than "because."

When a choice contains an "if," determine whether the entire statement is true, assuming that the proposition which follows the "if" is true.

There is no requirement that facts in the root of the question support the proposition following "if." There is no requirement for facts in the question to support the proposition that such a construction be reasonable.

"Because" or "if" need not be exclusive

There is no requirement for the conclusion following "if" or "because" to be exclusive.

For example, if a master could be liable in tort under the doctrine of *respondeat superior* or because the master was *negligent*, a choice using "if" or "because" holding the master liable would be correct if it stated either reason, even though the master might be liable for the other reason.

Exam tip for "because"

Notice that in an answer that would have been correct, the word "because" limits the facts you could consider to those in the body of the question containing specific facts.

The difference between the effect of "if" and "because" controls the answer.

Identify those limited situations (e.g., where the appropriate standard is strict liability) and distinguish them from those that are satisfactory (e.g., if the standard is negligence).

"Only if" requires exclusivity

Sometimes the words "only if" are used to distinguish between the two "affirmed" choices to make one wrong.

When an option uses the words "only if," assume that the entire proposition is correct as long as the words following "only if" are true.

The critical difference, where "only if" is used, is that the proposition cannot be true except when the condition is true. If there is another reason for the same result to be reached, the choice is wrong.

"Unless" questions

The conjunction "unless" has the same function as "only if," except that it precedes a negative exclusive condition instead of a positive exclusive condition.

It is essentially the mirror image of an "only if" choice.

For an option using "unless," reverse and substitute the words "only if" for "unless."

Limiting words

Choices can be made incorrect with limiting words that require that a proposition be true in all circumstances or under no circumstances.

Examples of limiting words include *all*, *any*, *never*, *always*, *only*, *every*, and *plenary*.

Notes for active learning

Making Correct Judgment Calls

Applying the law to the facts

Most questions give a fact pattern and ask which choice draws the correct legal conclusion required by the call of the question.

The first skill required is to draw inferences from facts given to place the conduct described in the question in the appropriate legal category.

The second skill is to apply the appropriate legal rule to conduct in that category and choose the option which reaches the appropriate conclusion.

The process of drawing inferences from a fact pattern and placing conduct in an appropriate category often requires judgment.

Bad judgment equals the wrong answer

To make the questions difficult, the examiners often place the conduct near the border of two different legal classifications.

Decide which side of the demarcation the conduct falls on. Inevitably, reasonable people can differ on these judgments.

If your judgment does not match the examiners, you will likely answer the question incorrectly, no matter how much law you know.

Mitigate this problem by reviewing released questions involving judgment calls where the examiners have published correct answers (i.e., their judgment call).

For example, a death occurring because the parties played Russian roulette is considered *depraved heart murder*, not *involuntary manslaughter*.

Judgment calls happen

Difficult judgment calls occur several times on the exam, and you are likely to make some close judgment calls incorrectly.

While this adds to the frustrations of multiple-choice tests, it is part of the exam.

By narrowing judgment call questions to two choices and guessing, you will get approximately half of them correct.

You will not fail the exam solely because you were unlucky on judgment calls.

The examiners remove many judgment calls by procedural devices.

The importance of procedure

The question may not ask what a jury should find on the facts.

The answer may be controlled by the procedural context of the criminal prosecution.

For example, it is given that the jury has found the defendant guilty of murder, and the only question on appeal is whether the judge should have granted a motion to dismiss at the end of hearing evidence. This is because a reasonable jury looking at the facts and inferences most favorable to the prosecution should not have found the defendant guilty of murder.

The same procedural issues exist when the question asks if a motion for summary judgment should be allowed or if the court should direct a verdict.

Exam Tips and Suggestions

Timing is everything

The time given to complete the exam is usually adequate if you practiced enough questions to improve speed and efficiency to the required level.

As you get closer to the test date, just doing practice questions is not enough.

You need to time your practice. Take previously released exams in two three-hour periods on the same day. Since these practice exams are approximately the same length as the exam, you will know if you have a timing problem.

If you do not practice under timed conditions, you risk exhausting time on the exam before answering all the questions.

Practice your timing under test-like conditions to know if the timing will be an issue. If you cannot complete the practice exam, you will have trouble with the exam.

If time is an issue, adjust your pace and continue practicing.

All questions do not require the same amount of time.

An approach for when time is not an issue

If you can complete 100 questions in three hours, use this strategy. At the start of the exam, break the allotted time into 15-minute intervals and write them down.

Set an initial pace of 9 questions every fifteen minutes.

Check your progress at each 15-minute interval.

If you completed 18 questions in the first half-hour, 36 in the first hour, 72 in the first two hours, and 90 in the first two and a half hours, you are on target to complete the exam on time. At this pace, you should complete 100 questions in two hours and forty-six minutes.

This leaves 14 minutes to check the answer sheet, revisit troublesome questions, or use the time to go a little slower on the last questions when fatigue impairs acuity.

If you find that your careful pace is faster than the budgeted 9 questions every 15 minutes, work at a faster pace, but use the extra time on the more challenging questions or in rechecking your work at the end.

Do *not* change the original answer choice unless you have a specific reason.

It is unwise to leave the exam early.

An approach for when time is an issue

During practice, continue answering questions to complete the section even after the time for self-paced exams has expired. Note which question you completed within the allocated time. Strive to complete the questions within the allotted time during your final exam prep.

If you learn from taking the practice test that you may not finish the questions in the allotted time on the actual exam, skip those questions with a long fact pattern followed by only one question. Keep your place on the answer sheet by skipping the row.

Return to those questions at the end and complete as many as time permits. Before turning your exam in, guess at the rest to reduce the number of random guesses.

Answer every question, even if you have not read the question, since wrong answers do *not* count against you.

Difficult questions

If you do not know the answer, do not spend a disproportionate amount of time on it since each question counts the same. Mark it in the test booklet, make a shrewd guess within the budgeted time and come back if time allows.

Do *not* leave questions unanswered. No points are deducted for wrong answers.

Minimize fatigue to maximize your score

The mental energy required to answer all the multiple-choice questions under stress produces fatigue (even with a lunch break).

Fatigue slows processing questions effectively and impairs reading comprehension. You may process questions more slowly at the end of each session and more quickly at the beginning before fatigue sets in.

Take at least two released exams under timed conditions to know how significantly fatigue affects your performance.

Be sure to arrive at the exam site on time. If necessary, stay at a nearby hotel rather than getting up early and risking a long drive the morning of the exam.

Relax during the lunch break and do not discuss the morning session with others.

You should know enough about your metabolism to eat the correct foods during the exam and reinforce appropriate caffeine levels if appropriate.

Proofread the answer sheet

As you decide on each correct answer, circle the corresponding letter in the exam book, and mark the appropriate block on the answer sheet.

The answer sheet is the only document graded by the examiners.

At the pace of 9 questions per 15 minutes, about 14 minutes should remain. Spend that time proofreading the answer sheet. Verify the answers circled to be certain that you marked the appropriate block on the answers.

Ensure that there are no blanks, and no questions have two answers.

Do *not* use this time to change an answer already selected unless you have a particularly good reason to change it.

If you have erased, ensure the erasure is thorough, or the computer may reject the answer because it cannot distinguish between marked answers.

If you have time after proofreading, review the problematic questions, and re-think the answers chosen. However, even after careful thought, hesitate to change an answer.

Do not leave any section of the exam early; use the allotted time wisely.

Intelligent preparation over a sustained period

There is no easy way to conquer an exam as challenging and comprehensive as the MBE, except through practice and an investment of time and effort well before the exam.

By diligently preparing, practicing questions, and intelligently assessing why questions were answered incorrectly, your skills for the exam will improve substantially.

Continue to improve those skills by following the advice given herein until reaching a proficiency level enabling you to pass the bar. This proficiency is accurately measured in multiple-choice format questions.

Some students will have to work harder to achieve the required proficiency.

The tools are in this study guide, and any law school graduate can be successful in passing the bar if they invest the required time and effort to be prepared.

Notes for active learning

Essay Preparation Strategies and Essay-Writing Suggestions

Memorize the law

Do not make the mistake of waiting too long before memorizing the governing law. Start learning the governing law early to be better prepared and pass the exam.

Memorize essential principles and focus on highly tested governing law.

Focus on the highly tested essay rules

Do not treat all subjects the same when you prepare for the essay portion of the exam.

Some governing law topics are tested more than others. It is crucial to focus on the highly tested topics (e.g., torts, contracts. property, civil procedure).

Know and apply enough governing laws to pass the bar – focus on commonly tested governing laws (e.g., negligence) provided in this book.

Practice writing essay answers each week

Practicing is crucial to a high score on essays. Practice regularly and avoid procrastination for this essential component of bar prep.

Incorporate practicing essay writing into your exam study schedule. To reduce procrastination, schedule time for writing practice essays each week.

For the MPT, practice by drafting full MPTs. Most examinees procrastinate on preparing for the MPT; there is nothing to memorize.

Do not make the *fatal mistake* of not practicing. The MPT portion is worth 20% of the UBE score.

Know the format and *practice that format to* increase your UBE score. This practice will increase your score and the probability of passing the bar.

Add one essay-specific subject each week

The Multistate Essay Exam (MEE) subjects include the 7 MBE subjects plus the 5 subjects of Business Associations (Agency, Partnerships, Corporations, and LLCs), Conflict of Laws, Family Law, Trusts and Estates, and Secured Transactions (UCC Article 9).

Combine highly tested subjects (e.g., torts) with less-tested subjects (e.g., secured transactions) and complex topics (e.g., contracts) with easier topics (e.g., business associations).

From preparation, know which subjects you struggle with and require a focused effort to master the essential governing law.

Make it easy for the grader to award points

Your answer to a question will probably be read in less than five minutes by a grader with a checklist to find that you have seen the issues and discussed them intelligently. Writing organized and clear answers makes it easy for the essay grader to award points.

Use headings for each of the major issues.

If the question suggests a structure for the answer because it is divided into parts or because the facts present a series of discrete issues, use the structure of the question, which is probably the structure of the checklist.

Use the IRAC method for the essay questions: state the issue, state the Rule. Apply the rule to the facts and conclude. IRAC seems simple, but following this approach makes it easier for the grader to know that you identified and addressed every issue and applied the law to the facts given.

IRAC results in more points during the exam.

Do not spend time trying to formulate eloquent issue statements. The question often outlines the issues, so an eloquent issue statement is redundant, and issue statements do not earn extra points.

Many examinees spend too much time developing an impressive issue statement and omit other essentials of their analysis (e.g., truncated analysis section).

An issue statement "Torts" or "Is the defendant liable for negligence?" is enough.

Do not waste time arguing both sides. There are no "two sides" for many essays to argue on bar essays because these are not law school essays.

Apply the law to facts and conclude unless asserting each party has good arguments.

Conclusion for each essay question

Points will be lost unless you conclude for each issue identified in the facts or are asked to address it in the call of the question.

Use caution starting the essay with the conclusion unless confident it is correct.

Many sample answers provided by the National Conference of Bar Examiners start with a definite and strong conclusion. Use caution to start with a conclusion unless confident (e.g., NCBE sample responses) your conclusion is correct.

Starting with a conclusion that is not correct draws attention to an incorrect conclusion at the start, which may influence the grader disproportionality. The grader may lose faith in your answer from the onset, and it is advisable to have a neutral heading rather than a firm conclusion that is wrong.

Tips for an easy-to-read essay

Use paragraph breaks between the Issue, Rule, Analysis, and Conclusion. Paragraph break makes it easy for the grader to read and score your essays. Additionally, this approach makes the answer appear longer and more complete.

Emphasize keywords and phrases. Underline key phrases so the grader notices that you addressed the governing law and applied it to the facts given.

After graders score several essays on the same topic, they scan essays for specific phrases that they expect to locate within a complete essay.

Think before you write

Read each question carefully to understand the facts and their necessary implications thoroughly and accurately.

After skimming the question, spend time on the focus line at the end of the question. Review the facts with the call of the question in mental focus.

Write a short outline of the issues raised. Outline in your mind the issues; state to yourself the tentative conclusions; test each conclusion from the standpoints of law and common sense; revise, as necessary.

Decide on a logical, orderly, and convincing arrangement for the response. Until then, you are not ready to write the answer.

Of the thirty-six minutes allotted to each essay, spend 15 minutes on issue spotting and organization and about twenty minutes writing the answer.

The ability to think and communicate like a lawyer

The Board knows that you have completed law school, under competent instructors, and have passed law school exams. The bar does not challenge the results of your law school courses.

The exam tests the ability to apply what you have learned to facts that might arise in practice and which, in some instances, involve several fields of law. The value of an answer depends not only on the correctness of the conclusions but on displaying essential legal principles and thinking like a lawyer.

Conclude on each issue presented. If a conclusion is derived from fuzzy facts, construct a well-reasoned argument supporting your conclusion to receive full credit regardless of if you conclude the same as the examiners.

If the correct answer depends on a provision of substantive law, which you are not familiar with, you can obtain a passing answer to the question by reaching a well-reasoned conclusion applying general law principles.

Do not try to limit the question to a particular subject area. Many questions combine traditional subjects, and you must be prepared to answer the question applying principles you learned across various subjects.

Do not restate the facts

The examiners know the facts; there is no time to waste. Do not restate the facts but use them to apply and integrate legal principles in writing the essay.

Do not fight the facts, particularly the focus line of the question.

For example, if the facts state that A executed a valid will, write about valid wills. If the question asks you to argue on behalf of A, do not argue on behalf of B because B has a prevailing argument. However, raise potential arguments which could be made on behalf of B and counter them in arguing on behalf of A.

Do not state abstract or irrelevant propositions of law

It is usually undesirable to begin an answer with a legal proposition. If the proposition is applicable, it will be more appropriate later to indicate the reason for your conclusion. If it is not applicable, do not state a surplus fact or legal principle.

Although it is seldom necessary to state an applicable rule of law in detail, make a sufficient reference to it so that the examiner appreciates your knowledge of the principle and conditions when it applies.

Do not, by speculating on different facts, nor in other ways, work into your answer some point of law with which you happen to be familiar, but which does not apply to the answer. Importantly, the examiners are not interested in knowing how many rules of law you know, but your ability to apply the applicable rules to the facts.

If the question says that A and B in the above hypothetical are unrelated, do not talk about the results which would occur if they were husband and wife.

Use the principles of law applicable to the call of the question and the facts. You must state the principles of applicable law to demonstrate to the examiner that you know the elements of the rule and how they apply to these facts.

For example, if the facts said that A transferred to B (a non-relative) the money necessary for B to purchase Blackacre from C and asks who owns Blackacre, you would say, "Since A furnished the consideration for the purchase of Blackacre and B took the title to the property in their name, B holds title to Blackacre in a resulting trust for A.

Do not detail the black letter law of resulting trusts since you have shown your knowledge by properly applying the facts to the law of resulting trusts.

Do not fight the facts and address a contrary fact not presented. The examiners may take points away if you make that mistake because you are not focused on the issues presented.

Discuss all the issues raised

A grasp of all the issues is essential.

For example, if there are three issues in a question, a discussion of only one issue, no matter how masterly, if coupled with omitting the others, could not result in 100% credit. It would probably result in a score of 33%.

The exam includes many issues in most questions so it can be graded mechanically. This maintains consistency across a group of several graders for each exam question.

The grader has a checklist of issues and awards most points for the examinee that identifies issues and intelligently discusses each.

Failure to see and discuss enough issues intelligently is probably the biggest reason for failure on the essay portion of the exam.

Methods for finding all issues

Use all the facts presented. Failure to discuss facts probably means that you missed important issues.

If you must decide in the early part of the question (e.g., does the court have jurisdiction) and you decide that issue so the remaining facts become irrelevant, make an alternative assumption ("If the court does have jurisdiction") and answer the question in the alternative using facts which would otherwise be irrelevant.

Do not avoid issues because you are not sure of the substantive law. If the examiners stated that X's nephew helped X escape after a crime, discuss the nephew's status as an accessory after the fact. If you do not know whether he is a close enough relative to be exempt under the statute, answer this issue by making alternative assumptions.

Indicators requiring alternative arguments

Ambiguous terms – if there are words in the fact pattern that are neutral or ambiguous such as "put up," the examiners look for possible interpretations of these terms.

Language in quotes – language placed in quotes is almost always ambiguous and must be construed as part of the answer.

Avoid ambiguous, rambling statements and verbosity

Generally, do not use compound sentences. Two separate sentences are preferred.

Complex sentences are particularly useful to apply the facts of the question to the applicable principle of law.

For example, in the previous resulting trust hypothetical, write, "Since B purchased Blackacre and took title in their name with money furnished by A, A holds title to Blackacre in a resulting trust, even if B has not signed a memorandum."

Avoid undue repetition

If the same principle of law and conclusion apply to two parts of an answer, state it once in detail, and refer back for the second part.

For example, if you have discussed A's liability and now must discuss B's liability, say, "B is also guilty of murder for the same reasons as A. (see discussion above)."

Avoid slang and colloquialism

The examiners judge your formal writing style.

If the examiner shows humor with names and events, do not show your sense of humor.

Use the standard abbreviations:

P for Plaintiff

D for Defendant

K for Contract

BFP for *Bona Fide* purchaser

Write legibly and coherently

Printing is usually easier to read than handwriting.

Use all the pages, and do not crowd your answer.

Plan your answer so that you do not have to use inserts and arrows.

Timing strategies

On the MEE, you must complete six equally weighted essay questions in three hours; an average of 30 minutes per question.

You have flexibility with time limitations as questions are not of the same difficulty.

There are two absolute figures:

spend no more than 45 minutes on any question,

spend at least 20 minutes on each question.

Be careful about not going over the time limit on the first question because this will require a readjustment of your timing for the entire session. If you miss the deadlines, re-divide your remaining time so that you will have an equal amount of time on each question.

If you go over by 15 minutes a question, do not allocate 30 minutes for other questions.

Stay focused

Do not start by reading the entire exam. Answer the questions in order and do not consider more than one question at a time.

After answering, put it out of your mind and not worry about your response. Keep your mind clear to focus on the next question.

Proofread your answers as time permits.

Law school essay grading matrix

An "A" answer is an outstanding response. It correctly and fully identifies dispositive issues and sub-issues raised by the question. The answer states the applicable legal rules and sub-rules with precision. It analyzes the question thoroughly with the applicable rules and explores alternative analysis where appropriate. It applies the law to the facts to conclude and is not cluttered by irrelevant matters. An "A" answer demonstrates an objectively superior mastering of the subject. An answer is not an "A" answer simply because it is better than most students' answers.

A "B" answer is a good response. It presents the four components of a good answer (issues, rules, analysis & application, and conclusion), but it does so in a way that could be improved. For example, it may be that not all critical issues have been spotted, or the issues are not presented clearly. The statement of legal rules captures that basic law but may not develop the law's complexities or nuances. The analysis is competent but lacks subtlety and may be somewhat simplistic or conclusory.

A "C" answer is a minimally competent response. It contains the four components of a good answer (issues, rules, analysis & application, and conclusion) but may not distinguish them. Perhaps only some issues have been identified while others are missed. The rules of law lack completeness or accuracy. The analysis and application may be shallow and conclusory. Conclusions may be questionable and not well-defended.

A "D" answer lacks basic components. It may identify the wrong issues or none. Rules are stated incorrectly. The analysis is conclusory or absent. The law is not applied to the facts coherently. Conclusions are unsupported or missing. The response exhibits a lack of knowledge of legal issues and rules or demonstrates an inability to engage in legal analysis.

Best wishes with your preparation!

Appendix

Overview of American Law

Overview of American Law

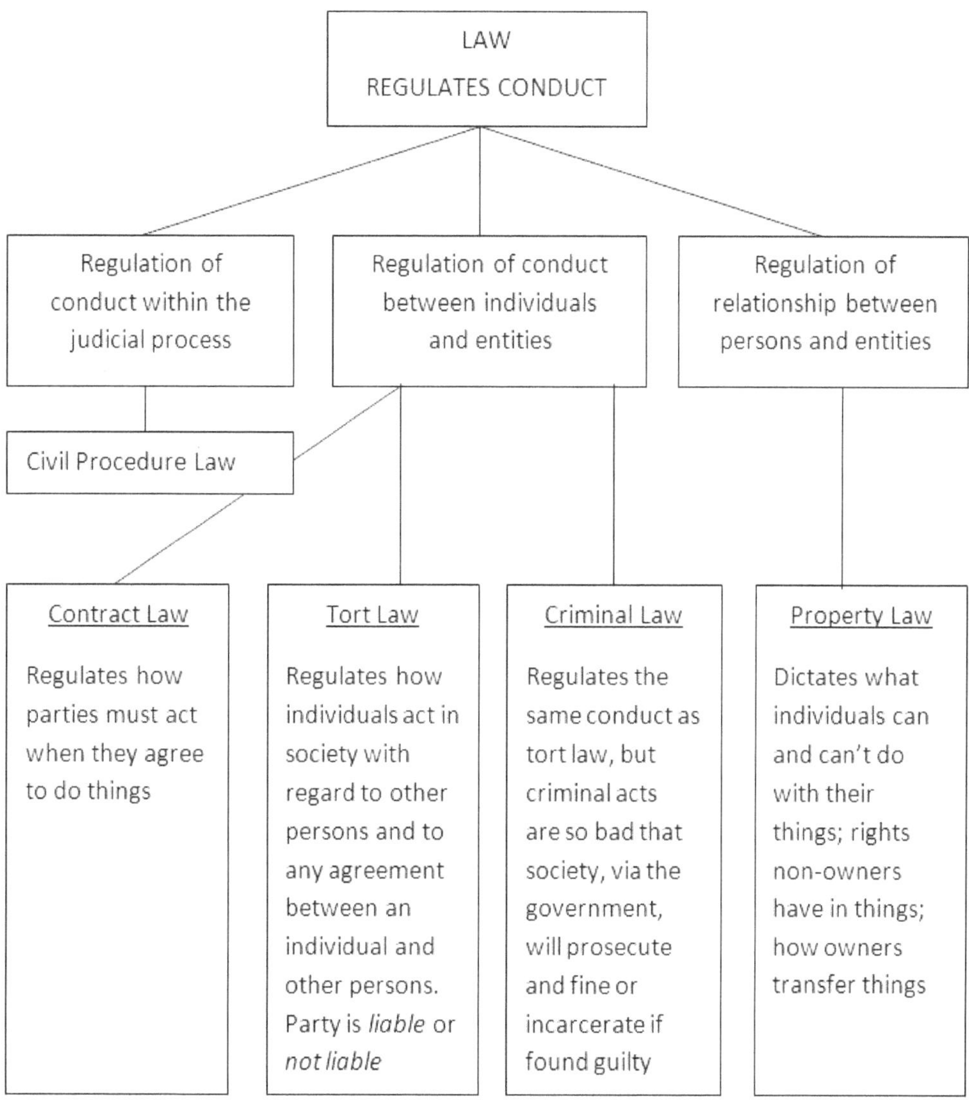

U.S. Court Systems – Federal and State Courts

There are two kinds of courts in the USA – federal courts and state courts.

Federal courts are established under the U.S. Constitution by Congress to decide disputes involving the Constitution and laws passed by Congress. A state establishes state and local courts (within states, local courts are established by cities, counties, and other municipalities).

Jurisdiction of federal and state courts

The differences between federal courts and state courts are defined by jurisdiction.[1] Jurisdiction refers to the kinds of cases that a particular court is authorized to hear and adjudicate (i.e., the pronouncement of a legally binding judgment upon the parties to the dispute).

Federal court jurisdiction is limited to the types of cases listed in the Constitution and specifically provided by Congress. For the most part, federal courts only hear:

- cases in which the United States is a party[2];

- cases involving violations of the U.S. Constitution or federal laws (under federal-question jurisdiction[3]);

- cases between citizens of different states if the amount in controversy *exceeds* $75,000 (under diversity jurisdiction[4]); and

- bankruptcy, copyright, patent, and maritime law cases.

State courts, in contrast, have broad jurisdiction, so the cases individual citizens are likely to be involved in (e.g., robberies, traffic violations, contracts, and family disputes) are usually heard and decided in state courts. The only cases state courts are not allowed to hear are lawsuits against the United States and those involving certain specific federal laws: criminal, antitrust, bankruptcy, patent, copyright, and some maritime law cases.

In many cases, both federal and state courts have jurisdiction whereby the plaintiff (i.e., the party initiating the suit) can choose whether to file their claim in state or federal court.

Criminal cases involving federal laws can be tried only in federal court, but most criminal cases involve violations of state law and are tried in state court. Robbery is a crime, but what law makes it is a crime? Except for certain exceptions, state laws, not federal laws, make robbery a crime. There are only a few federal laws about robbery, such as the law that makes it a federal crime to rob a bank whose deposits are insured by a federal agency. Examples of other federal crimes are the transport of illegal drugs into the country or across state lines and using the U.S. mail system to defraud consumers.

Crimes committed on federal property (e.g., national parks or military reservations) are prosecuted in federal court.

Federal courts may hear cases concerning state laws if the issue is whether the state law violates the federal Constitution. Suppose a state law forbids slaughtering animals outside of certain limited areas. A neighborhood association brings a case in state court against a defendant who sacrifices chickens in their backyard. When the court issues an order (i.e., an injunction[5]) forbidding the defendant from further sacrifices, the defendant challenges the state law in federal court as an unconstitutional infringement of religious freedom.

Some conduct is illegal under both federal and state laws. For example, federal laws prohibit employment discrimination, and the states have added additional legal restrictions. A person can file their claim in either federal or state court under federal law or federal and state laws. A case that only involves a state law can be brought only in state court.

Appeals for review of actions by federal administrative agencies are federal civil cases.

For example, if the Environmental Protection Agency, over the objection of area residents, issued a permit to a paper mill to discharge water used in its milling process into the Scenic River, the residents may appeal and have the federal court of appeals review the agency's decision.

[1] *jurisdiction* – 1) the legal authority of a court to hear and decide specific types of case; 2) the geographic area over which the court has the authority to decide cases.

[2] *parties* – the plaintiff and the defendant in a lawsuit.

[3] *federal-question jurisdiction* – the federal district courts' authorization to hear and decide cases arising under the Constitution, laws, or treaties of the United States.

[4] *diversity jurisdiction* – the federal district courts' authority to hear and decide civil cases involving plaintiffs and defendants who are citizens of different states (or U.S. citizens and foreign nationals) and meet specific statutory requirements.

[5] *injunction* – a judge's order that a party takes or refrain from taking a particular action. An injunction may be preliminary until the outcome of a case is determined or permanent.

Organization of the federal courts

Congress has divided the country into 94 federal judicial districts, with each having a U.S. district court. The U.S. district courts are the federal trial courts -- where federal cases are tried, witnesses testify, and juries serve.

Each district has a U.S. bankruptcy court, which is part of the district court that administers the U.S. bankruptcy laws.

Congress uses state boundaries to help define the districts. Some districts cover an entire state, like Idaho. Other districts cover just part of a state, like the Northern District of California. Congress placed each of the ninety-four districts in one of twelve regional circuits whereby each circuit has a court of appeals. The losing party can petition the court of appeals to review the case to determine if the district judge applied the law correctly.

There is a U.S. Court of Appeals for the Federal Circuit, whose jurisdiction is defined by subject matter rather than geography. It hears appeals from certain courts and agencies, such as the U.S. Court of International Trade, the U.S. Court of Federal Claims, and the U.S. Patent and Trademark Office, and certain types of cases from the district courts (mainly lawsuits claiming that patents have been infringed).

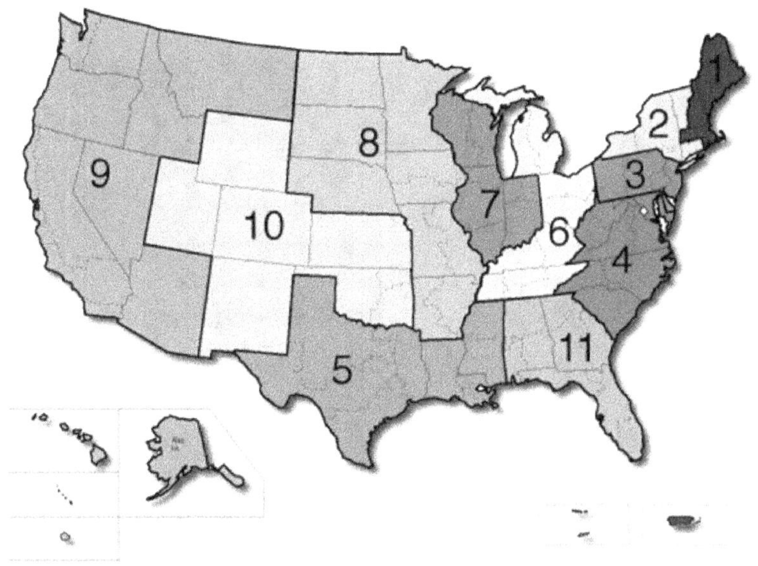

Twelve regional federal circuits

The Supreme Court in Washington, D.C., is the highest court in the nation. The losing party can petition in a case in the court of appeals (or, sometimes, in a state supreme court), can petition the Supreme Court to hear an appeal.

Unlike a court of appeals, the Supreme Court does not have to hear the case. The Supreme Court hears only a small percentage of the cases it is asked to review.

Notes for active learning

How Civil Cases Move Through the Federal Courts

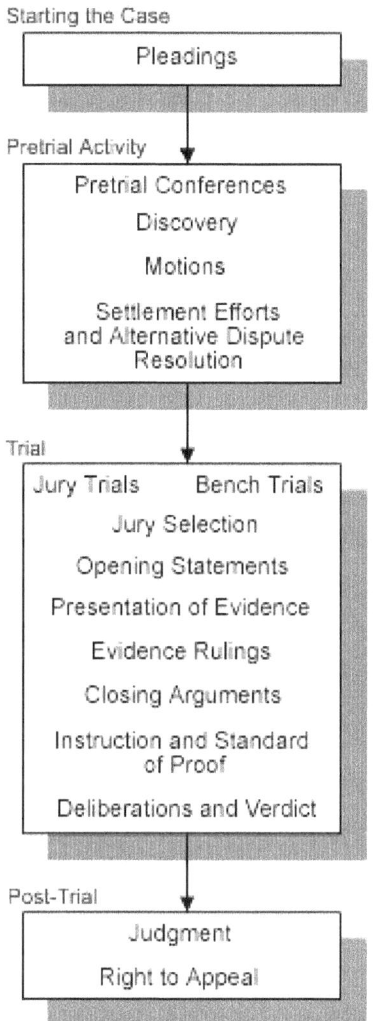

A federal civil case begins when a person, or their legal representative, files a paper with the clerk of the court that asserts another person's wrongful act injured the person. In legal terminology, the plaintiff files a *complaint* against the defendant.

The defendant files an *answer* to the complaint. These written statements of the party's positions are called pleadings. In some circumstances, the defendant may file a *motion* instead of an answer; the motion asks the court to take some action, such as dismiss the case or require the plaintiff to explain more clearly what the lawsuit is about.

Jury trials

In a jury trial, the jury decides what happened, and to apply the legal standards, the judge tells them to apply to reach a verdict. The plaintiff presents evidence supporting its view of the case, and the defendant presents evidence rebutting the plaintiff's evidence or supporting its view of the case. From these presentations, the jury must decide what happened and applied the law to those facts.

The jury never decides what law applies to the case; that is the role of the judge. For example, in a discrimination case where the plaintiff alleged that their workplace was hostile, the judge tells the jury the legal standard for a hostile environment.

The jury would have to decide whether the plaintiff's description of events was true and whether those events met the legal standard. A trial jury, or petit jury, may consist of six to twelve jurors in a civil case.

Bench trials

If the parties agree not to have a *jury trial* and leave the fact-finding to the judge, the trial is a *bench trial*. In bench and jury trials, the judge ensures the correct legal standards are followed.

In contrast to a jury trial, the judge decides the facts and renders the verdict in a *bench trial*.

For example, in a discrimination case in which the plaintiff alleged a hostile environment, the judge would determine the legal standard for a hostile environment and decide whether the plaintiff's description of events was true and whether those events met the legal standard.

Some kinds of cases always have bench trials. For example, there is never a jury trial if the plaintiff is seeking an injunction, an order from the judge that the defendant does, or stop doing something, as opposed to monetary damages.

Some statutes provide that a judge must decide the facts in certain types of cases.

Jury selection

A jury trial begins with the selection of jurors. Citizens are selected for jury service through a process set out in laws passed by Congress and in the federal rules of procedure.

First, citizens are called to court to be available to serve on juries. These citizens are selected at random from sources, in most districts, lists of registered voters, which may be augmented by other sources, such as lists of licensed drivers in the judicial district.

The judge and the lawyers choose who will serve on the jury.

To choose the jurors, the judge and sometimes the lawyers ask prospective jurors questions to determine if they will decide the case fairly, a process known as *voir dire*.

The lawyers may request that the judge excuse jurors they think may not be impartial, such as those who know a party in the case or who have had an experience that might make them favor one side over the other. These requests for rejecting jurors are *challenges for cause*.

The lawyers may request that the judge excuse a certain number of jurors without reason; these requests are *peremptory challenges*.

Instructions and standard of proof

Following the closing arguments, the judge gives instructions to the jury, explaining the relevant law, how the law applies to the case, and what questions the jury must decide.

How sure do jurors have to be before they reach a verdict? One important instruction the judge gives the jury is the standard of proof they must follow in deciding the case.

The courts, through their decisions, and Congress, through statutes, have established standards by which facts must be proven in criminal and civil cases.

In civil cases, to decide for the plaintiff, the jury must determine by a *preponderance of the evidence* that the defendant failed to perform a legal duty and violated the plaintiff's rights. A preponderance of the evidence means that, based on the evidence, the evidence favors the plaintiff more (even if only slightly) than it favors the defendant.

If the evidence in favor of the plaintiff could be placed on one side of a scale and that in favor of the defendant on the other, the plaintiff would win if the evidence in favor of the plaintiff was heavy enough to tip the scale. If the two sides were even, or if the scale tipped for the defendant, the defendant would win.

Judgment

In civil cases, if the jury (or judge) decides in favor of the plaintiff, the result usually is that the defendant must pay the plaintiff money or damages. The judge orders the defendant to pay the decided amount. Sometimes the defendant is ordered to take some specific action that will restore the plaintiff's rights. If the defendant wins the case, there is nothing more the trial court needs to do as the case is disposed of and the defendant is held not liable.

Right to appeal

The losing party in a federal civil case has a right to appeal the verdict to the U.S. court of appeals (i.e., Federal Circuit Courts) and ask the court to review the case to determine whether the trial was conducted properly. The losing party in the state trial court has a right to appeal the verdict to the state court of appeal.

The grounds for appeal usually are that the federal district (or state) judge made an error, either in the procedure (e.g., admitting improper evidence) or interpreting the law. The government may appeal in civil cases, as any other party may. Neither party may appeal if there was no trial -- parties settled their civil case out of court.

Notes for active learning

How Criminal Cases Move Through the Federal Courts

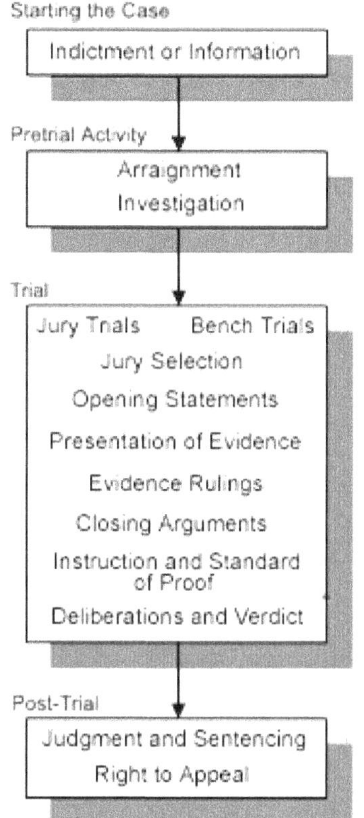

Indictment or information

A criminal case formally begins with an indictment or information, which is a formal accusation that a person committed a crime.

An indictment may be obtained when a lawyer (i.e., prosecutor) for the executive branch of the U.S. government (i.e., U.S. attorney or assistant U.S. attorney) present evidence to a federal grand jury that, according to the government, indicates a person committed a crime.

The U.S. attorney tries to convince the grand jury that there is enough evidence to show that the person probably committed the crime and should be formally accused. If the grand jury agrees, it issues an indictment.

A grand jury is different from a trial jury or petit jury.

A grand jury determines whether the person may be tried for a crime; a petit jury listens to the evidence presented at the trial and determines whether the defendant is guilty.

Petit is French for "small"; petit juries usually consist of twelve jurors in criminal cases.

Grand is French for "large"; grand juries have from sixteen to twenty-three jurors.

Grand jury indictments are most often used for *felonies* (i.e., punishable by imprisonment of more than a year or by death) such as bank robberies or sales of illegal drugs.

Grand jury indictments are not necessary to prosecute *misdemeanors* (i.e., less serious than a felony but more serious than an infraction) and are necessary for felonies.

For lesser crimes, the U.S. attorney issues an *information* that substitutes for an indictment. For example, speeding on a highway in a national park is a misdemeanor.

An information is used when a defendant waives an indictment by a grand jury.

Arraignment

After the grand jury issues the indictment, the accused (i.e., defendant) is summoned to court or arrested (if not already in custody). The next step is an arraignment, a proceeding in which the defendant is brought before a judge, told of the charges they are accused of, and asked to plead guilty or not guilty. If the defendant's plea is guilty, a time is set for the defendant to return to court to be sentenced.

If the defendant pleads "not guilty," the time is set for the trial.

A defendant may enter a plea bargain with the prosecution--usually by agreeing to plead guilty to some but not all charges or lesser charges. The prosecution drops the remaining charges.

About nine out of ten defendants in criminal cases plead guilty.

Investigation

In a criminal case, a defense lawyer conducts a thorough investigation before trial, interviewing witnesses, visiting the crime scene, and examining physical evidence. An important part of this investigation is determining whether the evidence the government plans to use to prove its case was obtained legally.

The Fourth Amendment to the Constitution forbids unreasonable searches and seizures. To enforce this protection, the Supreme Court has decided that illegally seized evidence cannot be used at trial for most purposes.

For example, if the police seize evidence from a defendant's home without a search warrant, the lawyer for the defendant can ask the court to exclude the evidence from use at trial. The court holds a hearing to determine whether the search was unreasonable.

If the court rules that key evidence was seized illegally and cannot be used, the government often drops the charges against the defendant.

If the government has a strong case and the court ruled that the evidence was obtained legally, the defendant may decide to plead guilty rather than go to trial, where a conviction is likely.

Deliberations and verdict

After receiving its instructions from the judge, the jury retires to the jury room to discuss the evidence and reach a verdict (a decision on the factual issues). A criminal jury verdict must be unanimous; all jurors must agree that the defendant is guilty or not guilty.

If the jurors cannot agree, the judge declares a mistrial, and the prosecutor must decide whether to ask the court to dismiss the case or have it presented to another jury.

Judgment and sentencing

In federal criminal cases, if the jury (or judge, if there is no jury) decides that the defendant is guilty, the judge sets a date for a sentencing hearing. In federal criminal cases, the jury does not decide whether the defendant will go to prison or for how long; the judge does.

In federal death penalty cases, the jury does decide whether the defendant will receive a death sentence. Sentencing statutes passed by Congress control the judge's sentencing decision. Additionally, judges use Sentencing Guidelines, issued by the U.S. Sentencing Commission, as a source of advice as to the proper sentence. The guidelines consider the nature of the offense and the offender's criminal history.

A presentence report, prepared by one of the court's probation officers, provides the judge with information about the offender and the offense, including the sentence recommended by the guidelines. After determining the sentence, the judge signs a judgment, including the plea, the verdict, and sentence.

Right to appeal

A defendant who is found guilty in a federal criminal trial has a right to appeal the decision to the U.S. court of appeals, that is, ask the court of appeals to review the case to determine whether the trial was conducted properly. The grounds for appeal are usually that the district judge is said to have made an error, either in a procedure (admitting improper evidence, for example) or interpreting the law.

A defendant who pled guilty may not appeal the conviction.

A defendant who pled guilty may have the right to appeal their sentence.

The government may not appeal if a defendant in a criminal case is found not guilty because the Double Jeopardy Clause of the Fifth Amendment to the Constitution provides that no person shall "be twice put in jeopardy of life or limb" for the same offense.

This reflects society's belief that, even if a subsequent trial might finally find a defendant guilty, it is not proper for the government to harass an acquitted defendant through repeated retrials.

However, the government may sometimes appeal a sentence.

Notes for active learning

How Civil and Criminal Appeals Move Through the Federal Courts

Assignment of Judges

Alternative Dispute Resolution (ADR)

Review of Lower Court Decision

Oral Argument

Decision

The Supreme Court of the United States

Assignment of judges

The courts of appeals usually assign cases to a panel of three judges. The panel decides the case for the entire court. Sometimes, when the parties request it or a question of unusual importance, the judges on the appeals court assemble *en banc* (a rare event).

Review of a lower court decision

In making its decision, the panel reviews key parts of the record. The record consists of the documents filed in the case at trial and the transcript of the trial proceedings. The panel learns about the lawyers' legal arguments from the lawyers' briefs.

Briefs are written documents that each side submits to explain its case and tell why the court should decide in its favor.

Oral argument

If the court permits oral argument, the lawyers for each side have a limited amount of time (typically between 15 to 30 minutes) to argue (i.e., advocate and explain) their case to the judges (or justices at the highest court in the jurisdiction) in a formal courtroom session. The judges (or justices for the highest court in the jurisdiction) frequently question the attorneys about the relevant law as it applies to the facts and issues in the case before them.

A court of appeals differs from the federal trial courts. There are no jurors, witnesses, or court reporters. The lawyers for each side, but not the parties, are usually present in the courtroom.

Decision

After the submission of briefs and oral arguments, the judges discuss the case privately, consider relevant *precedents* (court decisions from higher courts in prior cases with similar facts and legal issues), and reach a decision. Courts are required to follow precedents.

For example, a U.S. court of appeals must follow the U.S. Supreme Court's decisions; a district court must follow the decisions of the U.S. Supreme Court and the decisions of the court of appeals of its circuit.

Courts are influenced by decisions they are not required to follow, such as the decisions of other circuits. Courts follow precedent unless they set forth reasons for the diversion.

At least two of the three judges on the panel must agree on a decision. One judge who agrees with the decision is chosen to write an opinion, which announces and explains the decision.

If a judge on the panel disagrees with the majority's opinion, the judge may write a dissent, giving reasons for disagreeing.

Many appellate opinions are published in books of opinions, called reporters. The opinions are read carefully by other judges and lawyers looking for precedents to guide them in their cases.

The accumulated judicial opinions make up a body of law known as *case law*, which is usually an accurate predictor of how future cases will be decided.

For decisions that the judges believe are important to the parties and contribute little to the law, the appeals courts frequently use short, unsigned opinions that often are not published.

If the court of appeals decides that the trial judge incorrectly interpreted the law or followed incorrect procedures, it reverses the district court's decision.

For example, the court of appeals could hold that the district judge allowed the jury to base its decision on evidence that never should have been admitted, and thus the defendant cannot be guilty.

Most of the time, courts of appeals uphold, rather than the reverse, district court decisions.

Sometimes when a higher court reverses the decision of the district court, it sends the case back (i.e., *remand* the case) to the lower court for another trial.

For example, *Miranda v. Arizona* case (1966), the Supreme Court ruled 5-4 that Ernesto Miranda's confession could not be used as evidence because he had not been advised of his right to remain silent or of his right to have a lawyer present during questioning.

However, the government did have other evidence against him. The case was remanded for a new trial, in which the improperly obtained confession was not used as evidence, but the other evidence convicted Miranda.

The Supreme Court of the United States

The Supreme Court is the highest in the nation. It is a different kind of appeals court; its major function is not correcting errors made by trial judges but clarifying the law in cases of national importance or when lower courts disagree about interpreting the Constitution or federal laws.

The Supreme Court does not have to hear every case that it is asked to review. Each year, losing parties ask the Supreme Court to review about 8,000 cases.

Almost all cases come to the Court as a *petition for writ of certiorari*. The court selects only about 80 to 120 of the most significant cases to review with oral arguments.

Supreme Court decisions establish a precedent for interpreting the Constitution and federal laws; holdings that state and federal courts must follow.

The power of judicial review makes the Supreme Court's role in our government vital. Judicial review is the power of a court when deciding a case to declare that a law passed by a legislature or action by the executive branch is invalid because it is inconsistent with the Constitution.

Although district courts, courts of appeals, and state courts can exercise the power of judicial review, their decisions about federal law are always subject, on appeal, to review by the Supreme Court.

When the Supreme Court declares a law unconstitutional, its decision can only be overruled by a later decision of the Supreme Court or Amendment to the Constitution.

Seven of the twenty-seven Amendments to the Constitution have invalidated the decisions of the Supreme Court. However, most Supreme Court cases do not concern the constitutionality of laws, but the interpretation of laws passed by Congress.

Although Congress has steadily increased the number of district and appeals court judges over the years, the Supreme Court has remained the same size since 1869. It consists of a Chief Justice and eight associate justices.

Like the federal court of appeals and federal district judges, the Supreme Court justices are appointed by the President with the Senate's *advice and consent.*

Unlike the judges in the courts of appeals, Supreme Court justices never sit on panels. Absent recusal, nine justices hear cases, and a majority ruling decides cases.

The Supreme Court begins its annual session, or term, on the first Monday of October. The term lasts until the Court has announced its decisions in cases where it has heard an argument that term—usually late June or early July.

During the term, the Court, sitting for two weeks at a time, hears oral arguments on Monday through Wednesday and holds private conferences to discuss the cases, reach decisions, and begin preparing the written opinions that explain its decisions.

Most decisions and opinions are released in the late spring and early summer.

Standards of review for federal courts

Standard of review	De novo	Clearly erroneous	Abuse of discretion
Type of decision under review	Question of the law	Question of fact	Discretionary action
Lower-court decision maker	Trial judge	Trial judge	Trial judge
Deference given to lower court	No deference	Substantial deference	Extreme deference
Party typically benefitted	Appellant	Appellee	Appellee
Definition	An appellate court reviews the legal question anew and independently, without regard to the conclusions reached by the trial court. "When *de novo* review is compelled, no form of appellate deference is acceptable." *Salve Regina College v. Russell,* (1991).	A finding is 'clearly erroneous' when although there is evidence to support it, the reviewing court on the entire evidence is left with the definite and firm conviction that a mistake has been committed. *United States v. United States Gypsum Co.,* (1948) "If the district court's account of the evidence is plausible in light of the record viewed in its entirety, the court of appeals may not reverse it even though convinced that had it been sitting as the trier of fact, it would have weighed the evidence differently. When there are two permissible views of the evidence, the factfinder's choice between them cannot be clearly erroneous." *Anderson v. Bessemer City,* (1985).	Generally, an abuse of discretion only occurs where no reasonable person could take the view adopted by the trial court. If reasonable persons could differ, no abuse of discretion can be found. *Harrington v. DeVito,* (7th Cir.1981) Under the abuse of discretion standard, a trial court's decision will not be disturbed unless the appellate court has a definite and firm conviction that the lower court made a clear error of judgment or exceeded the bounds of permissible choice in the circumstances. We will not alter a trial court's decision unless it can be shown that the court's decision was an arbitrary, capricious, whimsical, or manifestly unreasonable judgment. *Wright v. Abbott Laboratories, Inc.,* (10th Cir. 2001)
Examples	Motions for summary judgment, constitutional questions, statutory interpretation	Questions regarding who did what, where, and when; questions of intent and motive; questions of ultimate fact (such as negligence)	Rule 11 sanctions, attorney's fees, courtroom management, motions to compel, injunctions, and temporary restraining orders.

The Constitution of the United States (*a transcription*)

THE U.S. NATIONAL ARCHIVES & RECORDS ADMINISTRATION
www.archives.gov

The following text is a transcription of the Constitution as it was inscribed by Jacob Shallus on parchment (the document on display in the Rotunda at the National Archives Museum.) The spelling and punctuation reflect the original.

The Constitution of the United States: A Transcription

The following text is a transcription of the Constitution as it was inscribed by Jacob Shallus on parchment (displayed in the Rotunda at the National Archives Museum.) The authenticated text of the Constitution can be found on the website of the Government Printing Office.

We the People of the United States, in Order to form a more perfect Union, establish Justice, insure domestic Tranquility, provide for the common defence, promote the general Welfare, and secure the Blessings of Liberty to ourselves and our Posterity, do ordain and establish this Constitution for the United States of America.

Article. I

Section. 1.

All legislative Powers herein granted shall be vested in a Congress of the United States, which shall consist of a Senate and House of Representatives.

Section. 2.

The House of Representatives shall be composed of Members chosen every second Year by the People of the several States, and the Electors in each State shall have the Qualifications requisite for Electors of the most numerous Branch of the State Legislature.

No Person shall be a Representative who shall not have attained to the Age of twenty five Years, and been seven Years a Citizen of the United States, and who shall not, when elected, be an Inhabitant of that State in which he shall be chosen.

Representatives and direct Taxes shall be apportioned among the several States which may be included within this Union, according to their respective Numbers, which shall be determined by adding to the whole Number of free Persons, including those bound to Service for a Term of Years, and excluding Indians not taxed, three fifths of all other Persons. The actual Enumeration shall be made within three Years after the first Meeting of the Congress of the United States, and within every subsequent Term of ten Years, in such Manner as they shall by Law direct. The Number of Representatives shall not exceed one for every thirty Thousand, but each State shall have at Least one Representative; and until such enumeration shall be made, the State of New Hampshire shall be entitled to chuse three, Massachusetts eight, Rhode-Island and Providence

Plantations one, Connecticut five, New-York six, New Jersey four, Pennsylvania eight, Delaware one, Maryland six, Virginia ten, North Carolina five, South Carolina five, and Georgia three.

When vacancies happen in the Representation from any State, the Executive Authority thereof shall issue Writs of Election to fill such Vacancies.

The House of Representatives shall chuse their Speaker and other Officers; and shall have the sole Power of Impeachment.

Section. 3.

The Senate of the United States shall be composed of two Senators from each State, chosen by the Legislature thereof, for six Years; and each Senator shall have one Vote.

Immediately after they shall be assembled in Consequence of the first Election, they shall be divided as equally as may be into three Classes. The Seats of the Senators of the first Class shall be vacated at the Expiration of the second Year, of the second Class at the Expiration of the fourth Year, and of the third Class at the Expiration of the sixth Year, so that one third may be chosen every second Year; and if Vacancies happen by Resignation, or otherwise, during the Recess of the Legislature of any State, the Executive thereof may make temporary Appointments until the next Meeting of the Legislature, which shall then fill such Vacancies.

No Person shall be a Senator who shall not have attained to the Age of thirty Years, and been nine Years a Citizen of the United States, and who shall not, when elected, be an Inhabitant of that State for which he shall be chosen.

The Vice President of the United States shall be President of the Senate, but shall have no Vote, unless they be equally divided.

The Senate shall chuse their other Officers, and also a President pro tempore, in the Absence of the Vice President, or when he shall exercise the Office of President of the United States.

The Senate shall have the sole Power to try all Impeachments. When sitting for that Purpose, they shall be on Oath or Affirmation. When the President of the United States is tried, the Chief Justice shall preside: And no Person shall be convicted without the Concurrence of two thirds of the Members present.

Judgment in Cases of Impeachment shall not extend further than to removal from Office, and disqualification to hold and enjoy any Office of honor, Trust or Profit under the United States: but the Party convicted shall nevertheless be liable and subject to Indictment, Trial, Judgment and Punishment, according to Law.

Section. 4.

The Times, Places and Manner of holding Elections for Senators and Representatives, shall be prescribed in each State by the Legislature thereof; but the Congress may at any time by Law make or alter such Regulations, except as to the Places of chusing Senators.

The Congress shall assemble at least once in every Year, and such Meeting shall be on the first Monday in December, unless they shall by Law appoint a different Day.

Section. 5.

Each House shall be the Judge of the Elections, Returns and Qualifications of its own Members, and a Majority of each shall constitute a Quorum to do Business; but a smaller Number may adjourn from day to day, and may be authorized to compel the Attendance of absent Members, in such Manner, and under such Penalties as each House may provide.

Each House may determine the Rules of its Proceedings, punish its Members for disorderly Behaviour, and, with the Concurrence of two thirds, expel a Member.

Each House shall keep a Journal of its Proceedings, and from time to time publish the same, excepting such Parts as may in their Judgment require Secrecy; and the Yeas and Nays of the Members of either House on any question shall, at the Desire of one fifth of those Present, be entered on the Journal.

Neither House, during the Session of Congress, shall, without the Consent of the other, adjourn for more than three days, nor to any other Place than that in which the two Houses shall be sitting.

Section. 6.

The Senators and Representatives shall receive a Compensation for their Services, to be ascertained by Law, and paid out of the Treasury of the United States. They shall in all Cases, except Treason, Felony and Breach of the Peace, be privileged from Arrest during their Attendance at the Session of their respective Houses, and in going to and returning from the same; and for any Speech or Debate in either House, they shall not be questioned in any other Place.

No Senator or Representative shall, during the Time for which he was elected, be appointed to any civil Office under the Authority of the United States, which shall have been created, or the Emoluments whereof shall have been encreased during such time; and no Person holding any Office under the United States, shall be a Member of either House during his Continuance in Office.

Section. 7.

All Bills for raising Revenue shall originate in the House of Representatives; but the Senate may propose or concur with Amendments as on other Bills.

Every Bill which shall have passed the House of Representatives and the Senate, shall, before it become a Law, be presented to the President of the United States; If he approves he shall sign it, but if not he shall return it, with his Objections to that House in which it shall have originated, who shall enter the Objections at large on their Journal, and proceed to reconsider it. If after such Reconsideration two thirds of that House shall agree to pass the Bill, it shall be sent, together with the Objections, to the other House, by which it shall likewise be reconsidered, and if approved by two thirds of that House, it shall become a Law. But in all such Cases the Votes of both Houses shall be determined by yeas and Nays, and the Names of the Persons voting for and against the Bill shall be entered on the Journal of each House respectively. If any Bill shall not be returned by the President within ten Days (Sundays excepted) after it shall have been presented to him, the Same shall be a Law, in like Manner as if he had signed it, unless the Congress by their Adjournment prevent its Return, in which Case it shall not be a Law.

Every Order, Resolution, or Vote to which the Concurrence of the Senate and House of Representatives may be necessary (except on a question of Adjournment) shall be presented to the President of the United States; and before the Same shall take Effect, shall be approved by him, or being disapproved by him, shall be repassed by two thirds of the Senate and House of Representatives, according to the Rules and Limitations prescribed in the Case of a Bill.

Section. 8.

The Congress shall have Power To lay and collect Taxes, Duties, Imposts and Excises, to pay the Debts and provide for the common Defence and general Welfare of the United States; but all Duties, Imposts and Excises shall be uniform throughout the United States;

To borrow Money on the credit of the United States;

To regulate Commerce with foreign Nations, and among the several States, and with the Indian Tribes;

To establish an uniform Rule of Naturalization, and uniform Laws on the subject of Bankruptcies throughout the United States;

To coin Money, regulate the Value thereof, and of foreign Coin, and fix the Standard of Weights and Measures;

To provide for the Punishment of counterfeiting the Securities and current Coin of the United States;

To establish Post Offices and post Roads;

To promote the Progress of Science and useful Arts, by securing for limited Times to Authors and Inventors the exclusive Right to their respective Writings and Discoveries;

To constitute Tribunals inferior to the Supreme Court;

To define and punish Piracies and Felonies committed on the high Seas, and Offences against the Law of Nations;

To declare War, grant Letters of Marque and Reprisal, and make Rules concerning Captures on Land and Water;

To raise and support Armies, but no Appropriation of Money to that Use shall be for a longer Term than two Years;

To provide and maintain a Navy;

To make Rules for the Government and Regulation of the land and naval Forces;

To provide for calling forth the Militia to execute the Laws of the Union, suppress Insurrections and repel Invasions;

To provide for organizing, arming, and disciplining, the Militia, and for governing such Part of them as may be employed in the Service of the United States, reserving to the States respectively, the Appointment of the Officers, and the Authority of training the Militia according to the discipline prescribed by Congress;

To exercise exclusive Legislation in all Cases whatsoever, over such District (not exceeding ten Miles square) as may, by Cession of particular States, and the Acceptance of Congress, become the Seat of the Government of the United States, and to exercise like Authority over all Places purchased by the Consent of the Legislature of the State in which the Same shall be, for the Erection of Forts, Magazines, Arsenals, dock-Yards, and other needful Buildings;—And

To make all Laws which shall be necessary and proper for carrying into Execution the foregoing Powers, and all other Powers vested by this Constitution in the Government of the United States, or in any Department or Officer thereof.

Section. 9.

The Migration or Importation of such Persons as any of the States now existing shall think proper to admit, shall not be prohibited by the Congress prior to the Year one thousand eight hundred and eight, but a Tax or duty may be imposed on such Importation, not exceeding ten dollars for each Person.

The Privilege of the Writ of Habeas Corpus shall not be suspended, unless when in Cases of Rebellion or Invasion the public Safety may require it.

No Bill of Attainder or ex post facto Law shall be passed.

No Capitation, or other direct, Tax shall be laid, unless in Proportion to the Census or enumeration herein before directed to be taken.

No Tax or Duty shall be laid on Articles exported from any State.

No Preference shall be given by any Regulation of Commerce or Revenue to the Ports of one State over those of another: nor shall Vessels bound to, or from, one State, be obliged to enter, clear, or pay Duties in another.

No Money shall be drawn from the Treasury, but in Consequence of Appropriations made by Law; and a regular Statement and Account of the Receipts and Expenditures of all public Money shall be published from time to time.

No Title of Nobility shall be granted by the United States: And no Person holding any Office of Profit or Trust under them, shall, without the Consent of the Congress, accept of any present, Emolument, Office, or Title, of any kind whatever, from any King, Prince, or foreign State.

Section. 10.

No State shall enter into any Treaty, Alliance, or Confederation; grant Letters of Marque and Reprisal; coin Money; emit Bills of Credit; make any Thing but gold and silver Coin a Tender in Payment of Debts; pass any Bill of Attainder, ex post facto Law, or Law impairing the Obligation of Contracts, or grant any Title of Nobility.

No State shall, without the Consent of the Congress, lay any Imposts or Duties on Imports or Exports, except what may be absolutely necessary for executing it's inspection Laws: and the net

Produce of all Duties and Imposts, laid by any State on Imports or Exports, shall be for the Use of the Treasury of the United States; and all such Laws shall be subject to the Revision and Controul of the Congress.

No State shall, without the Consent of Congress, lay any Duty of Tonnage, keep Troops, or Ships of War in time of Peace, enter into any Agreement or Compact with another State, or with a foreign Power, or engage in War, unless actually invaded, or in such imminent Danger as will not admit of delay.

Article. II

Section. 1.

The executive Power shall be vested in a President of the United States of America. He shall hold his Office during the Term of four Years, and, together with the Vice President, chosen for the same Term, be elected, as follows

Each State shall appoint, in such Manner as the Legislature thereof may direct, a Number of Electors, equal to the whole Number of Senators and Representatives to which the State may be entitled in the Congress: but no Senator or Representative, or Person holding an Office of Trust or Profit under the United States, shall be appointed an Elector.

The Electors shall meet in their respective States, and vote by Ballot for two Persons, of whom one at least shall not be an Inhabitant of the same State with themselves. And they shall make a List of all the Persons voted for, and of the Number of Votes for each; which List they shall sign and certify, and transmit sealed to the Seat of the Government of the United States, directed to the President of the Senate. The President of the Senate shall, in the Presence of the Senate and House of Representatives, open all the Certificates, and the Votes shall then be counted. The Person having the greatest Number of Votes shall be the President, if such Number be a Majority of the whole Number of Electors appointed; and if there be more than one who have such Majority, and have an equal Number of Votes, then the House of Representatives shall immediately chuse by Ballot one of them for President; and if no Person have a Majority, then from the five highest on the List the said House shall in like Manner chuse the President. But in chusing the President, the Votes shall be taken by States, the Representation from each State having one Vote; A quorum for this Purpose shall consist of a Member or Members from two thirds of the States, and a Majority of all the States shall be necessary to a Choice. In every Case, after the Choice of the President, the Person having the greatest Number of Votes of the Electors shall be the Vice President. But if there should remain two or more who have equal Votes, the Senate shall chuse from them by Ballot the Vice President.

The Congress may determine the Time of chusing the Electors, and the Day on which they shall give their Votes; which Day shall be the same throughout the United States.

No Person except a natural born Citizen, or a Citizen of the United States, at the time of the Adoption of this Constitution, shall be eligible to the Office of President; neither shall any Person be eligible to that Office who shall not have attained to the Age of thirty five Years, and been fourteen Years a Resident within the United States.

In Case of the Removal of the President from Office, or of his Death, Resignation, or Inability to discharge the Powers and Duties of the said Office, the Same shall devolve on the Vice President, and the Congress may by Law provide for the Case of Removal, Death, Resignation or Inability, both of the President and Vice President, declaring what Officer shall then act as President, and such Officer shall act accordingly, until the Disability be removed, or a President shall be elected.

The President shall, at stated Times, receive for his Services, a Compensation, which shall neither be encreased nor diminished during the Period for which he shall have been elected, and he shall not receive within that Period any other Emolument from the United States, or any of them.

Before he enters on the Execution of his Office, he shall take the following Oath or Affirmation:—"I do solemnly swear (or affirm) that I will faithfully execute the Office of President of the United States, and will to the best of my Ability, preserve, protect and defend the Constitution of the United States."

Section. 2.

The President shall be Commander in Chief of the Army and Navy of the United States, and of the Militia of the several States, when called into the actual Service of the United States; he may require the Opinion, in writing, of the principal Officer in each of the executive Departments, upon any Subject relating to the Duties of their respective Offices, and he shall have Power to grant Reprieves and Pardons for Offences against the United States, except in Cases of Impeachment.

He shall have Power, by and with the Advice and Consent of the Senate, to make Treaties, provided two thirds of the Senators present concur; and he shall nominate, and by and with the Advice and Consent of the Senate, shall appoint Ambassadors, other public Ministers and Consuls, Judges of the supreme Court, and all other Officers of the United States, whose Appointments are not herein otherwise provided for, and which shall be established by Law: but the Congress may by Law vest the Appointment of such inferior Officers, as they think proper, in the President alone, in the Courts of Law, or in the Heads of Departments.

The President shall have Power to fill up all Vacancies that may happen during the Recess of the Senate, by granting Commissions which shall expire at the End of their next Session.

Section. 3.

He shall from time to time give to the Congress Information of the State of the Union, and recommend to their Consideration such Measures as he shall judge necessary and expedient; he may, on extraordinary Occasions, convene both Houses, or either of them, and in Case of Disagreement between them, with Respect to the Time of Adjournment, he may adjourn them to such Time as he shall think proper; he shall receive Ambassadors and other public Ministers; he shall take Care that the Laws be faithfully executed, and shall Commission all the Officers of the United States.

Section. 4.

The President, Vice President and all civil Officers of the United States, shall be removed from Office on Impeachment for, and Conviction of, Treason, Bribery, or other high Crimes and Misdemeanors.

Article III

Section. 1.

The judicial Power of the United States, shall be vested in one supreme Court, and in such inferior Courts as the Congress may from time to time ordain and establish. The Judges, both of the supreme and inferior Courts, shall hold their Offices during good Behaviour, and shall, at stated Times, receive for their Services, a Compensation, which shall not be diminished during their Continuance in Office.

Section. 2.

The judicial Power shall extend to all Cases, in Law and Equity, arising under this Constitution, the Laws of the United States, and Treaties made, or which shall be made, under their Authority;—to all Cases affecting Ambassadors, other public Ministers and Consuls;—to all Cases of admiralty and maritime Jurisdiction;—to Controversies to which the United States shall be a Party;—to Controversies between two or more States;—between a State and Citizens of another State,—between Citizens of different States,—between Citizens of the same State claiming Lands under Grants of different States, and between a State, or the Citizens thereof, and foreign States, Citizens or Subjects.

In all Cases affecting Ambassadors, other public Ministers and Consuls, and those in which a State shall be Party, the supreme Court shall have original Jurisdiction. In all the other Cases before mentioned, the supreme Court shall have appellate Jurisdiction, both as to Law and Fact, with such Exceptions, and under such Regulations as the Congress shall make.

The Trial of all Crimes, except in Cases of Impeachment, shall be by Jury; and such Trial shall be held in the State where the said Crimes shall have been committed; but when not committed within any State, the Trial shall be at such Place or Places as the Congress may by Law have directed.

Section. 3.

Treason against the United States, shall consist only in levying War against them, or in adhering to their Enemies, giving them Aid and Comfort. No Person shall be convicted of Treason unless on the Testimony of two Witnesses to the same overt Act, or on Confession in open Court.

The Congress shall have Power to declare the Punishment of Treason, but no Attainder of Treason shall work Corruption of Blood, or Forfeiture except during the Life of the Person attainted.

Article. IV

Section. 1.

Full Faith and Credit shall be given in each State to the public Acts, Records, and judicial Proceedings of every other State. And the Congress may by general Laws prescribe the Manner in which such Acts, Records and Proceedings shall be proved, and the Effect thereof.

Section. 2.

The Citizens of each State shall be entitled to all Privileges and Immunities of Citizens in the several States.

A Person charged in any State with Treason, Felony, or other Crime, who shall flee from Justice, and be found in another State, shall on Demand of the executive Authority of the State from which he fled, be delivered up, to be removed to the State having Jurisdiction of the Crime.

No Person held to Service or Labour in one State, under the Laws thereof, escaping into another, shall, in Consequence of any Law or Regulation therein, be discharged from such Service or Labour, but shall be delivered up on Claim of the Party to whom such Service or Labour may be due.

Section. 3.

New States may be admitted by the Congress into this Union; but no new State shall be formed or erected within the Jurisdiction of any other State; nor any State be formed by the Junction of two or more States, or Parts of States, without the Consent of the Legislatures of the States concerned as well as of the Congress.

The Congress shall have Power to dispose of and make all needful Rules and Regulations respecting the Territory or other Property belonging to the United States; and nothing in this Constitution shall be so construed as to Prejudice any Claims of the United States, or of any particular State.

Section. 4.

The United States shall guarantee to every State in this Union a Republican Form of Government, and shall protect each of them against Invasion; and on Application of the Legislature, or of the Executive (when the Legislature cannot be convened), against domestic Violence.

Article. V

The Congress, whenever two thirds of both Houses shall deem it necessary, shall propose Amendments to this Constitution, or, on the Application of the Legislatures of two thirds of the several States, shall call a Convention for proposing Amendments, which, in either Case, shall be valid to all Intents and Purposes, as Part of this Constitution, when ratified by the Legislatures of three fourths of the several States, or by Conventions in three fourths thereof, as the one or the other Mode of Ratification may be proposed by the Congress; Provided that no Amendment which may be made prior to the Year One thousand eight hundred and eight shall in any Manner affect the first and fourth Clauses in the Ninth Section of the first Article; and that no State, without its Consent, shall be deprived of its equal Suffrage in the Senate.

Article. VI

All Debts contracted and Engagements entered into, before the Adoption of this Constitution, shall be as valid against the United States under this Constitution, as under the Confederation.

This Constitution, and the Laws of the United States which shall be made in Pursuance thereof; and all Treaties made, or which shall be made, under the Authority of the United States, shall be the supreme Law of the Land; and the Judges in every State shall be bound thereby, any Thing in the Constitution or Laws of any State to the Contrary notwithstanding.

The Senators and Representatives before mentioned, and the Members of the several State Legislatures, and all executive and judicial Officers, both of the United States and of the several States, shall be bound by Oath or Affirmation, to support this Constitution; but no religious Test shall ever be required as a Qualification to any Office or public Trust under the United States.

Article. VII

The Ratification of the Conventions of nine States, shall be sufficient for the Establishment of this Constitution between the States so ratifying the Same.

The Word, "the," being interlined between the seventh and eighth Lines of the first Page, The Word "Thirty" being partly written on an Erazure in the fifteenth Line of the first Page, The Words "is tried" being interlined between the thirty second and thirty third Lines of the first Page and the Word "the" being interlined between the forty third and forty fourth Lines of the second Page.

Attest William Jackson Secretary, done in Convention by the Unanimous Consent of the States present the Seventeenth Day of September in the Year of our Lord one thousand seven hundred and Eighty seven and of the Independance of the United States of America the Twelfth In witness whereof We have hereunto subscribed our Names, G°. Washington, *Presidt and deputy from Virginia*

Delaware
Geo: Read
Gunning Bedford jun
John Dickinson
Richard Bassett
Jaco: Broom

Maryland
James McHenry
Dan of St Thos.
Jenifer
Danl. Carroll

Virginia
John Blair
James Madison Jr.

North Carolina
Wm. Blount
Richd. Dobbs Spaight
Hu Williamson

South Carolina
J. Rutledge
Charles Cotesworth Pinckney
Charles Pinckney
Pierce Butler

Georgia
William Few
Abr Baldwin

New Hampshire
John Langdon
Nicholas Gilman

Massachusetts
Nathaniel Gorham
Rufus King

Connecticut
Wm. Saml. Johnson
Roger Sherman

New York
Alexander Hamilton

New Jersey
Wil: Livingston
David Brearley
Wm. Paterson
Jona: Dayton

Pensylvania
B Franklin
Thomas Mifflin
Robt. Morris
Geo. Clymer
Thos. FitzSimons
Jared Ingersoll
James Wilson
Gouv Morris

Enactment of the Bill of Rights of the United States of America (1791)

The first ten Amendments to the Constitution make up the Bill of Rights. Written by James Madison in response to calls from several states for greater constitutional protection for individual liberties, the Bill of Rights lists specific prohibitions on governmental power. The Virginia Declaration of Rights, written by George Mason, strongly influenced Madison.

One of the contention points between Federalists and Anti-Federalists was the Constitution's lack of a bill of rights that would place specific limits on government power.

Federalists argued that the Constitution did not need a bill of rights because the people and the states kept powers not explicitly given to the federal government.

Anti-Federalists held that a *bill of rights* was necessary to safeguard individual liberty.

Madison, then a member of the U.S. House of Representatives, went through the Constitution itself, making changes where he thought most appropriate.

Several Representatives, led by Roger Sherman, objected that Congress had no authority to change the wording of the Constitution. Therefore, Madison's changes were presented as a list of amendments that would follow Article VII.

The House approved 17 amendments. Of these 17, the Senate approved 12. Those 12 were sent to the states for approval in August of 1789. Of those 12 proposed amendments, 10 were quickly ratified. Virginia's legislature became the last to ratify the Amendments on December 15, 1791. These Amendments are the Bill of Rights.

The Bill of Rights is a list of limits on government power. For example, what the Founders saw as the natural right of individuals to speak and worship freely was protected by the First Amendment's prohibitions on Congress from making laws establishing a religion or abridging freedom of speech.

Another example is the natural right to be free from the government's unreasonable intrusion in one's home was safeguarded by the Fourth Amendment's warrant requirements.

Other precursors to the Bill of Rights include English documents such as the Magna Carta[1], the Petition of Rights, the English Bill of Rights, and the Massachusetts Body of Liberties.

The Magna Carta illustrates Compact Theory[1] as well as initial strides toward limited government. Its provisions address individual rights and political rights. Latin for "Great Charter," the Magna Carta was written by Barons in Runnymede, England, and forced on the King.

Although the protections were generally limited to the prerogatives of the Barons, the Magna Carta embodied the general principle that the King accepted limitations on his rule. These included the fundamental acknowledgment that the king was not above the law.

Included in the Magna Carta are protections for the English church, petitioning the king, freedom from the forced quarter of troops and unreasonable searches, due process and fair trial protections, and freedom from excessive fines. These protections can be found in the First, Third, Fourth, Fifth, Sixth, and Eighth Amendments to the Constitution.

The Magna Carta is the oldest compact in England. The Mayflower Compact, the Fundamental Orders of Connecticut, and the Albany Plan are examples from the American colonies.

The Articles of Confederation was a compact among the states, and the Constitution creates a compact based on a federal system between the national government, state governments, and the people. The Hayne-Webster Debate focused on the compact created by the Constitution.

[1] Philosophers including Thomas Hobbes, John Locke, and Jean-Jacques Rousseau theorized that peoples' condition in a "state of nature" (that is, outside of society) is one of freedom, but that freedom inevitably degrades into war, chaos, or debilitating competition without the benefit of a system of laws and government. They reasoned, therefore, that for their happiness, individuals willingly trade some of their natural freedom in exchange for the protections provided by the government.

The Bill of Rights: Amendments I–X

Amendment I

Congress shall make no law respecting an establishment of religion, or prohibiting the free exercise thereof; or abridging the freedom of speech, or of the press; or the right of the people peaceably to assemble, and to petition the government for a redress of grievances.

Amendment II

A well regulated militia, being necessary to the security of a free state, the right of the people to keep and bear arms, shall not be infringed.

Amendment III

No soldier shall, in time of peace be quartered in any house, without the consent of the owner, nor in time of war, but in a manner to be prescribed by law.

Amendment IV

The right of the people to be secure in their persons, houses, papers, and effects, against unreasonable searches and seizures, shall not be violated, and no warrants shall issue, but upon probable cause, supported by oath or affirmation, and particularly describing the place to be searched, and the persons or things to be seized.

Amendment V

No person shall be held to answer for a capital, or otherwise infamous crime, unless on a presentment or indictment of a grand jury, except in cases arising in the land or naval forces, or in the militia, when in actual service in time of war or public danger; nor shall any person be subject for the same offense to be twice put in jeopardy of life or limb; nor shall be compelled in any criminal case to be a witness against himself, nor be deprived of life, liberty, or property, without due process of law; nor shall private property be taken for public use, without just compensation.

Amendment VI

In all criminal prosecutions, the accused shall enjoy the right to a speedy and public trial, by an impartial jury of the state and district wherein the crime shall have been committed, which district shall have been previously ascertained by law, and to be informed of the nature and cause of the accusation; to be confronted with the witnesses against him; to have compulsory process for obtaining witnesses in his favor, and to have the assistance of counsel for his defense.

Amendment VII

In suits at common law, where the value in controversy shall exceed twenty dollars, the right of trial by jury shall be preserved, and no fact tried by a jury, shall be otherwise reexamined in any court of the United States, than according to the rules of the common law.

　　

Amendment VIII

Excessive bail shall not be required, nor excessive fines imposed, nor cruel and unusual punishments inflicted.

Amendment IX

The enumeration in the Constitution, of certain rights, shall not be construed to deny or disparage others retained by the people.

Amendment X

The powers not delegated to the United States by the Constitution, nor prohibited by it to the states, are reserved to the states respectively, or to the people.

Constitutional Amendments XI–XXVII

AMENDMENT XI

Passed by Congress March 4, 1794. Ratified February 7, 1795.

Note: Article III, section 2, of the Constitution was modified by amendment 11.

The Judicial power of the United States shall not be construed to extend to any suit in law or equity, commenced or prosecuted against one of the United States by Citizens of another State, or by Citizens or Subjects of any Foreign State.

AMENDMENT XII

Passed by Congress December 9, 1803. Ratified June 15, 1804.

Note: A portion of Article II, section 1 of the Constitution was superseded by the 12th amendment.

The Electors shall meet in their respective states and vote by ballot for President and Vice-President, one of whom, at least, shall not be an inhabitant of the same state with themselves; they shall name in their ballots the person voted for as President, and in distinct ballots the person voted for as Vice-President, and they shall make distinct lists of all persons voted for as President, and of all persons voted for as Vice-President, and of the number of votes for each, which lists they shall sign and certify, and transmit sealed to the seat of the government of the United States, directed to the President of the Senate; -- the President of the Senate shall, in the presence of the Senate and House of Representatives, open all the certificates and the votes shall then be counted; -- The person having the greatest number of votes for President, shall be the President, if such number be a majority of the whole number of Electors appointed; and if no person have such majority, then from the persons having the highest numbers not exceeding three on the list of those voted for as President, the House of Representatives shall choose immediately, by ballot, the President. But in choosing the President, the votes shall be taken by states, the representation from each state having one vote; a quorum for this purpose shall consist of a member or members from two-thirds of the states, and a majority of all the states shall be necessary to a choice. [And if the House of Representatives shall not choose a President whenever the right of choice shall devolve upon them, before the fourth day of March next following, then the Vice-President shall act as President, as in case of the death or other constitutional disability of the President. --]* The person having the greatest number of votes as Vice-President, shall be the Vice-President, if such number be a majority of the whole number of Electors appointed, and if no person have a majority, then from the two highest numbers on the list, the Senate shall choose the Vice-President; a quorum for the purpose shall consist of two-thirds of the whole number of Senators, and a majority of the whole number shall be necessary to a choice. But no person constitutionally ineligible to the office of President shall be eligible to that of Vice-President of the United States.

**Superseded by section 3 of the 20th Amendment.*

AMENDMENT XIII

Passed by Congress January 31, 1865. Ratified December 6, 1865.

Note: A portion of Article IV, section 2, of the Constitution was superseded by the 13th amendment.

Section 1.
Neither slavery nor involuntary servitude, except as a punishment for crime whereof the party shall have been duly convicted, shall exist within the United States, or any place subject to their jurisdiction.

Section 2.
Congress shall have power to enforce this article by appropriate legislation.

AMENDMENT XIV

Passed by Congress June 13, 1866. Ratified July 9, 1868.

Note: Article I, section 2, of the Constitution was modified by section 2 of the 14th amendment.

Section 1.
All persons born or naturalized in the United States, and subject to the jurisdiction thereof, are citizens of the United States and of the State wherein they reside. No State shall make or enforce any law which shall abridge the privileges or immunities of citizens of the United States; nor shall any State deprive any person of life, liberty, or property, without due process of law; nor deny to any person within its jurisdiction the equal protection of the laws.

Section 2.
Representatives shall be apportioned among the several States according to their respective numbers, counting the whole number of persons in each State, excluding Indians not taxed. But when the right to vote at any election for the choice of electors for President and Vice-President of the United States, Representatives in Congress, the Executive and Judicial officers of a State, or the members of the Legislature thereof, is denied to any of the male inhabitants of such State, being twenty-one years of age,* and citizens of the United States, or in any way abridged, except for participation in rebellion, or other crime, the basis of representation therein shall be reduced in the proportion which the number of such male citizens shall bear to the whole number of male citizens twenty-one years of age in such State.

Section 3.
No person shall be a Senator or Representative in Congress, or elector of President and Vice-President, or hold any office, civil or military, under the United States, or under any State, who, having previously taken an oath, as a member of Congress, or as an officer of the United States, or as a member of any State legislature, or as an executive or judicial officer of any State, to support the Constitution of the United States, shall have engaged in insurrection or rebellion against the same, or given aid or comfort to the enemies thereof. But Congress may by a vote of two-thirds of each House, remove such disability.

Section 4.

The validity of the public debt of the United States, authorized by law, including debts incurred for payment of pensions and bounties for services in suppressing insurrection or rebellion, shall not be questioned. But neither the United States nor any State shall assume or pay any debt or obligation incurred in aid of insurrection or rebellion against the United States, or any claim for the loss or emancipation of any slave; but all such debts, obligations and claims shall be held illegal and void.

Section 5.

The Congress shall have the power to enforce, by appropriate legislation, the provisions of this article.

Changed by section 1 of the 26th Amendment.

AMENDMENT XV

Passed by Congress February 26, 1869. Ratified February 3, 1870.

Section 1.

The right of citizens of the United States to vote shall not be denied or abridged by the United States or by any State on account of race, color, or previous condition of servitude.

Section 2.

The Congress shall have the power to enforce this article by appropriate legislation.

AMENDMENT XVI

Passed by Congress July 2, 1909. Ratified February 3, 1913.

Note: Article I, section 9, of the Constitution was modified by amendment 16.

The Congress shall have power to lay and collect taxes on incomes, from whatever source derived, without apportionment among the several States, and without regard to any census or enumeration.

AMENDMENT XVII

Passed by Congress May 13, 1912. Ratified April 8, 1913.

Note: Article I, section 3, of the Constitution was modified by the 17th Amendment.

The Senate of the United States shall be composed of two Senators from each State, elected by the people thereof, for six years; and each Senator shall have one vote. The electors in each State shall have the qualifications requisite for electors of the most numerous branch of the State legislatures.

When vacancies happen in the representation of any State in the Senate, the executive authority of such State shall issue writs of election to fill such vacancies: *Provided,* That the legislature of any State may empower the executive thereof to make temporary appointments until the people fill the vacancies by election as the legislature may direct.

This amendment shall not be so construed as to affect the election or term of any Senator chosen before it becomes valid as part of the Constitution.

AMENDMENT XVIII

Passed by Congress December 18, 1917. Ratified January 16, 1919. Repealed by Amendment 21.

Section 1.

After one year from the ratification of this article the manufacture, sale, or transportation of intoxicating liquors within, the importation thereof into, or the exportation thereof from the United States and all territory subject to the jurisdiction thereof for beverage purposes is hereby prohibited.

Section 2.

The Congress and the several States shall have concurrent power to enforce this article by appropriate legislation.

Section 3.

This article shall be inoperative unless it shall have been ratified as an amendment to the Constitution by the legislatures of the several States, as provided in the Constitution, within seven years from the date of the submission hereof to the States by the Congress.

AMENDMENT XIX

Passed by Congress June 4, 1919. Ratified August 18, 1920.

The right of citizens of the United States to vote shall not be denied or abridged by the United States or by any State on account of sex.

Congress shall have power to enforce this article by appropriate legislation.

AMENDMENT XX

Passed by Congress March 2, 1932. Ratified January 23, 1933.

Note: Article I, section 4, of the Constitution was modified by section 2 of this Amendment. In addition, a portion of the 12th Amendment was superseded by section 3.

Section 1.

The terms of the President and the Vice President shall end at noon on the 20th day of January, and the terms of Senators and Representatives at noon on the 3d day of January, of the years in which such terms would have ended if this article had not been ratified; and the terms of their successors shall then begin.

Section 2.

The Congress shall assemble at least once in every year, and such meeting shall begin at noon on the 3d day of January, unless they shall by law appoint a different day.

Section 3.

If, at the time fixed for the beginning of the term of the President, the President elect shall have died, the Vice President elect shall become President. If a President shall not have been chosen before the time fixed for the beginning of his term, or if the President elect shall have failed to qualify, then the Vice President elect shall act as President until a President shall have qualified; and the Congress may by law provide for the case wherein neither a President elect nor a Vice President elect shall have qualified, declaring who shall then act as President, or the manner in which one who is to act shall be selected, and such person shall act accordingly until a President or Vice President shall have qualified.

Section 4.

The Congress may by law provide for the case of the death of any of the persons from whom the House of Representatives may choose a President whenever the right of choice shall have devolved upon them, and for the case of the death of any of the persons from whom the Senate may choose a Vice President whenever the right of choice shall have devolved upon them.

Section 5.

Sections 1 and 2 shall take effect on the 15th day of October following the ratification of this article.

Section 6.

This article shall be inoperative unless it shall have been ratified as an amendment to the Constitution by the legislatures of three-fourths of the several States within seven years from the date of its submission.

AMENDMENT XXI

Passed by Congress February 20, 1933. Ratified December 5, 1933.

Section 1.

The eighteenth article of amendment to the Constitution of the United States is hereby repealed.

Section 2.

The transportation or importation into any State, Territory, or possession of the United States for delivery or use therein of intoxicating liquors, in violation of the laws thereof, is hereby prohibited.

Section 3.

This article shall be inoperative unless it shall have been ratified as an amendment to the Constitution by conventions in the several States, as provided in the Constitution, within seven years from the date of the submission hereof to the States by the Congress.

AMENDMENT XXII

Passed by Congress March 21, 1947. Ratified February 27, 1951.

Section 1.

No person shall be elected to the office of the President more than twice, and no person who has held the office of President, or acted as President, for more than two years of a term to which some other person was elected President shall be elected to the office of the President more than once. But this Article shall not apply to any person holding the office of President when this Article was proposed by the Congress, and shall not prevent any person who may be holding the office of President, or acting as President, during the term within which this Article becomes operative from holding the office of President or acting as President during the remainder of such term.

Section 2.

This article shall be inoperative unless it shall have been ratified as an amendment to the Constitution by the legislatures of three-fourths of the several States within seven years from the date of its submission to the States by the Congress.

AMENDMENT XXIII

Passed by Congress June 16, 1960. Ratified March 29, 1961.

Section 1.

The District constituting the seat of Government of the United States shall appoint in such manner as the Congress may direct:

A number of electors of President and Vice President equal to the whole number of Senators and Representatives in Congress to which the District would be entitled if it were a State, but in no event more than the least populous State; they shall be in addition to those appointed by the States, but they shall be considered, for the purposes of the election of President and Vice President, to be electors appointed by a State; and they shall meet in the District and perform such duties as provided by the twelfth article of amendment.

Section 2.

The Congress shall have power to enforce this article by appropriate legislation.

AMENDMENT XXIV

Passed by Congress August 27, 1962. Ratified January 23, 1964.

Section 1.

The right of citizens of the United States to vote in any primary or other election for President or Vice President, for electors for President or Vice President, or for Senator or Representative in Congress, shall not be denied or abridged by the United States or any State by reason of failure to pay any poll tax or other tax.

Section 2.

The Congress shall have power to enforce this article by appropriate legislation.

AMENDMENT XXV

Passed by Congress July 6, 1965. Ratified February 10, 1967.

Note: Article II, section 1, of the Constitution was affected by the 25th amendment.

Section 1.

In case of the removal of the President from office or of his death or resignation, the Vice President shall become President.

Section 2.

Whenever there is a vacancy in the office of the Vice President, the President shall nominate a Vice President who shall take office upon confirmation by a majority vote of both Houses of Congress.

Section 3.

Whenever the President transmits to the President pro tempore of the Senate and the Speaker of the House of Representatives his written declaration that he is unable to discharge the powers and duties of his office, and until he transmits to them a written declaration to the contrary, such powers and duties shall be discharged by the Vice President as Acting President.

Section 4.

Whenever the Vice President and a majority of either the principal officers of the executive departments or of such other body as Congress may by law provide, transmit to the President pro tempore of the Senate and the Speaker of the House of Representatives their written declaration that the President is unable to discharge the powers and duties of his office, the Vice President shall immediately assume the powers and duties of the office as Acting President.

Thereafter, when the President transmits to the President pro tempore of the Senate and the Speaker of the House of Representatives his written declaration that no inability exists, he shall resume the powers and duties of his office unless the Vice President and a majority of either the principal officers of the executive department or of such other body as Congress may by law provide, transmit within four days to the President pro tempore of the Senate and the Speaker of the House of Representatives their written declaration that the President is unable to discharge the powers and duties of his office. Thereupon Congress shall decide the issue, assembling within forty-eight hours for that purpose if not in session. If the Congress, within twenty-one days after receipt of the latter written declaration, or, if Congress is not in session, within twenty-one days after Congress is required to assemble, determines by two-thirds vote of both Houses that the President is unable to discharge the powers and duties of his office, the Vice President shall continue to discharge the same as Acting President; otherwise, the President shall resume the powers and duties of his office.

AMENDMENT XXVI

Passed by Congress March 23, 1971. Ratified July 1, 1971.

Note: Amendment 14, section 2, of the Constitution was modified by section 1 of the 26th amendment.

Section 1.
The right of citizens of the United States, who are eighteen years of age or older, to vote shall not be denied or abridged by the United States or by any State on account of age.

Section 2.
The Congress shall have power to enforce this article by appropriate legislation.

AMENDMENT XXVII

Originally proposed Sept. 25, 1789. Ratified May 7, 1992.

No law, varying the compensation for the services of the Senators and Representatives, shall take effect, until an election of Representatives shall have intervened

States' Rights Under the U.S. Constitution

Selective incorporation under the 14th Amendment

The U.S. Constitution has Articles and Amendments that established constitutional rights.

The provisions in the Bill of Rights (i.e., the first ten Amendments to the Constitution) were initially binding upon only the federal government.

In time, most of these provisions became binding upon the states through *selective incorporation* into the *due process clause* of the 14th Amendment (i.e., reverse incorporation).

When a provision is made binding on a state, a state can no longer restrict the rights guaranteed in that provision.

The 1st Amendment guarantees the freedoms of speech, press, religion, and assembly.

The 5th Amendment protects the right to grand jury proceedings in federal criminal cases.

The 6th Amendment guarantees a right to confront witnesses (i.e., Confrontation Clause).

The right to confront witnesses was not *selectively incorporated* into the due process clause of the 14th Amendment and is not binding upon the states.

Therefore, persons involved in state criminal proceedings as a defendant have no federal constitutional right to grand jury proceedings.

Whether an individual has a right to a grand jury becomes a question of state law.

The 10th Amendment, which is part of the **Bill of Rights**, was ratified on December 15, 1791. It states the Constitution's principle of **federalism** by providing that powers not granted to the **federal government** by the Constitution, nor prohibited to the **States**, are reserved to the States or the people.

Federalism in the United States

Federalism in the United States is the evolving relationship between **state governments** and the **federal government**.

The American government has evolved from a system of dual federalism to associative federalism.

In "Federalist No. 46," James Madison wrote that the states and national government "are in fact but different agents and trustees of the people, constituted with different powers."

Alexander Hamilton, in "Federalist No. 28," suggested that both levels of government would exercise authority to the citizens' benefit: "If their [the peoples'] rights are invaded by either, they can make use of the other as the instrument of redress."[3]

Because the states were preexisting political entities, the U.S. Constitution did not need to define or explain federalism in one section, but it often mentions the rights and responsibilities of state governments and state officials in relation to the federal government.

The federal government has certain *express powers* (also called *enumerated powers*), which are powers spelled out in the Constitution, including the right to levy taxes, declare war, and regulate interstate and foreign commerce.

Also, the *Necessary and Proper Clause* gives the federal government the *implied power* to pass any law "necessary and proper" to execute its express powers.

Enumerated powers of the Federal Government are contained in Article I, Section 8 of the U.S. Constitution.

Other powers—the *reserved powers*—are reserved to the people or the states under the 10th Amendment. The Supreme Court decision significantly expanded the power delegated to the federal government in *McCulloch v. Maryland* (1819) and the 13th, 14th and 15th, Amendments to the Constitution following the **Civil War.**

Comprehensive Glossary of Legal Terms

Over 2,100 essential legal terms defined and explained. An excellent reference source for law students, practitioners and readers seeking an understanding of legal vocabulary and its application.

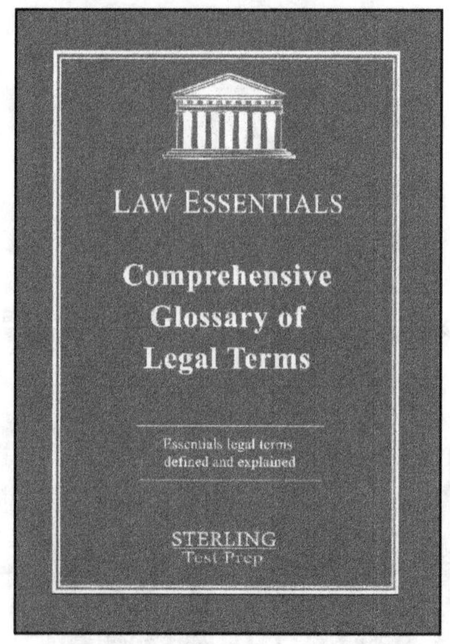

Landmark U.S. Supreme Court Cases: Essential Summaries

Learn important constitutional cases that shaped American law. Understand how the evolving needs of society intersect with the U.S. Constitution. Short summaries of seminal Supreme Court cases focused on issues and holdings.

Visit our Amazon store

Frank J. Addivinola, Ph.D., J.D., L.LM., MBA

The lead author and chief editor of this preparation guide is Dr. Frank Addivinola. With his outstanding education, professional training, legal and business experience, and university teaching, Dr. Addivinola lent his expertise to develop this book.

Attorney Frank Addivinola is admitted to practice law in several jurisdictions. He has served as an academic advisor and mentor for students and practitioners.

Dr. Addivinola holds an undergraduate degree from Williams College. He completed his Masters at Harvard University, Masters in Biotechnology at Johns Hopkins University, Masters in Technology Management and MBA at the University of Maryland University College, J.D. and L.LM. from Suffolk University, and Ph.D. in Law and Public Policy from Northeastern University.

During his extensive teaching career, Dr. Addivinola taught university courses in Introduction to Law and developed law coursebooks. He received several awards for community service, research, and presentations.